A Note From Rick Renner

I am on a personal quest to see a "revival of the Bible" so people can establish their lives on a firm foundation that will stand strong and endure the test as the end-time storm winds begin to intensify.

In order to experience a revival of the Bible in your personal life, it is important to take time each day to read, receive, and apply its truths to your life. James tells us that if we will continue in the perfect law of liberty — refusing to be forgetful hearers but determined to be doers — we will be blessed in our ways. As you watch or listen to the programs in this series and work through this corresponding study guide, I trust that you will search the Scriptures and allow the Holy Spirit to help you hear something new from God's Word that applies specifically to your life. I encourage you to be a doer of the Word that He reveals to you. Whatever the cost, I assure you — it will be worth it.

> Thy words were found, and I did eat them;
> and thy word was unto me the joy and rejoicing of mine heart:
> for I am called by thy name, O Lord God of hosts.
> — Jeremiah 15:16

Your brother and friend in Jesus Christ,

Rick Renner

Rick Renner

The Holy Spirit and You

Copyright © 2021 by Rick Renner
8316 E. 73rd St.
Tulsa, Oklahoma 74133

Published by Rick Renner Ministries
www.renner.org

ISBN 13: 978-1-6803-1873-9

eBook ISBN 13: 978-1-6803-1874-6

How To Use This Study Guide

This ten-lesson study guide corresponds to *"The Holy Spirit and You" With Rick Renner* (Renner TV). Each lesson in this study guide covers a topic that is addressed during the program series, with questions and references supplied to draw you deeper into your own private study of the Scriptures on this subject.

To derive the most benefit from this study guide, consider the following:

First, watch or listen to the program prior to working through the corresponding lesson in this guide. (Programs can also be viewed at **renner.org** by clicking on the Media/Archives links.)

Second, take the time to look up the scriptures included in each lesson. Prayerfully consider their application to your own life.

Third, use a journal or notebook to make note of your answers to each lesson's Study Questions and Practical Application challenges.

Fourth, invest specific time in prayer and in the Word of God to consult with the Holy Spirit. Write down the scriptures or insights He reveals to you.

Finally, take action! Whatever the Lord tells you to do according to His Word, do it.

For added insights on this subject, it is recommended that you obtain Rick Renner's book *The Holy Spirit and You: Working Together as Heaven's Dynamic Duo.* You may also select from Rick's other available resources by placing your order at **renner.org** or by calling 1-800-742-5593.

TOPIC

The Deeper Dimension

SCRIPTURES

Matthew 5:6 — Blessed are they which do hunger and thirst after righteousness: for they shall be filled.

GREEK WORDS

There are no Greek words for this lesson.

SYNOPSIS

The ten lessons in this study on *The Holy Spirit and You* will focus on the following topics:

- The Deeper Dimension
- The Holy Spirit, Our Comforter
- Being Led By the Holy Spirit
- The Holy Spirit Comforts and Indwells
- The Holy Spirit Teaches, Reminds, and Testifies
- The Holy Spirit Convicts and Convinces
- The Holy Spirit Guides
- The Holy Spirit Reveals and Helps Us To Worship
- The Holy Spirit Can Be Grieved
- The Desire of the Holy Spirit

The emphasis of this lesson:

There is a deeper dimension of spiritual living that can only be experienced by fully embracing the Person of the Holy Spirit and allowing Him to operate in your life. This was Jesus' existence — partnering with the Holy Spirit from conception to resurrection. If you are dissatisfied and spiritually hungry, let it drive you to a supernatural encounter with God.

Countless Christians go to church week after week — faithfully serving others, reading their Bibles, praying, and giving their tithes and offerings. They never miss a service, and yet it just seems like something is missing. All the while they're hoping that someday everything they have heard and been taught will begin to click and make sense to them. That's where Rick Renner was early on in his faith.

The Bible says that we overcome the enemy by the blood of the Lamb and the word of our testimony (*see* Revelation 12:11). In this first lesson, Rick shares his testimony of how he experienced a time of insatiable hunger for more of God and discovered a deeper dimension of living in divine partnership with the Holy Spirit.

RICK'S TESTIMONY

'I came to a place of deep dissatisfaction and spiritual hunger.'

"I was raised in a denominational church and saved at an early age. My family and I attended church whenever the doors were opened — Sunday morning, Sunday night, and a midweek service on Wednesday. My pastor was a very good Bible teacher, and he laid a spiritual feast in front of us at every gathering. Honestly, I am who I am today because of the solid, biblical foundation my pastor laid.

"But there came a point in my walk with God when intellectual information about Him was not enough. Something was missing. I felt as though there was a hole in the pit of my stomach, but I wasn't sure what it was. I began thinking, *There must be more to the Christian life than what I'm experiencing!*

"Although our church did a remarkable job at teaching the Bible, there was one aspect of Scripture that was not taught, and that's the present-day ministry of the Holy Spirit. Our church belonged to a denomination that would be considered *cessationists*, which means we didn't believe in the gifts of the Holy Spirit operating today. We believed that the supernatural gifts of the Holy Spirit *ceased* or came to an end with the death of the apostles.

"Again, I had grown up in a wonderful, Bible-believing church, but we didn't allow the Holy Spirit much room to operate except for in isolated moments like the invitation for people to surrender their lives to Christ at the end of the service. If there was one thing we did superbly, it was allowing the Holy Spirit to convict people of sin during the altar call. But that was about all we let Him do.

"Doctrinally and intellectually, I understood a great deal about the work of the Holy Spirit at that time in my life. I had been taught the truth about the Holy Spirit working to produce the character of God — and the fruit of the Spirit in us — conforming us to the image of Jesus Christ. And while that teaching was marvelous, it was primarily in the mental realm. It never put me in touch with the Holy Spirit's power in a real, tangible way. Experientially, I didn't know much about the Holy Spirit, and I yearned to know more.

"Everyone destined to grow in God eventually comes to a place of dissatisfaction in his or her spiritual life. Jesus said, 'Blessed are they which do hunger and thirst after righteousness: for they shall be filled' (Matthew 5:6). Interestingly, the original Greek text of this verse says, 'Blessed are they who are *hungering* and *thirsting*,' which indicates an ongoing condition that can be a prolonged period of time. People who are spiritually hungry are blessed because their spiritual hunger and thirst will lead them to a new encounter with God.

"Oftentimes seasons of spiritual hunger that precede a new infilling can be one of the most miserable a person will ever face. I experienced this firsthand. I began to ask questions of my Sunday school teachers and leaders that I was told I was 'not supposed to ask,' and they would quickly shut me down. Amazingly, this state of spiritual misery drives a person to a position where God reveals Himself to him or her in a more powerful way."

'I began asking questions about the Holy Spirit.'

"I had an aunt who had become Pentecostal, and although we all loved her, we saw her as one who had strayed away from the true faith. In our view, Pentecostals were involved in emotionalism and off balance, so we kind of stayed at a distance from my aunt. Nevertheless, on one particular day in 1973, I decided to drop by her house to say hello. In those days, no one locked their doors. And since the front door was unlocked, I went right in.

"At that time, she was working in another room of the house while listening to an old reel-to-reel teaching tape by Kenneth E. Hagin. Now, I didn't have a clue who Kenneth Hagin was, but I was strangely drawn in to the message he was teaching. As Brother Hagin was speaking, suddenly he began to give a message in tongues. Then someone interpreted the tongues. I still remember standing there in my aunt's living room in a state of shock with my mouth hanging open.

"*That's tongues,* I thought to myself. *I'm listening to tongues. This is what my church has warned me against, and here I am listening to it.*

"About that time, my aunt came around the corner and into the living room. The moment she saw me, she was stunned, and her eyes became as big as saucers. She knew my parents would not be happy about me hearing someone speaking in tongues, yet that is exactly what I heard as I stood motionless in her living room.

"After that experience, I began asking questions about the Holy Spirit. Every day after school, I would go to my aunt's house and engage in deep conversations about the infilling of the Holy Spirit. I was determined to know everything I could about Him. Instead of being offended or afraid, I was intrigued and magnetically drawn to know more.

"Today, there are some charismatic churches that work hard to tone down the gifts of the Spirit because they are afraid people will be offended. The truth is, many people today are hungry for the supernatural and they are doing everything they can to seek it out. So instead of squelching the gifts of the Holy Spirit, we need to parade the gifts. These supernatural manifestations are what attract people to the power of God. It's certainly what attracted me."

'It was as if the Jesus of the gospels stepped onto the stage and began healing people.'

"One day as I was flipping from one radio station to the next, I came across a program that completely captivated me. It was *Kathryn Kuhlman.* I was fascinated with how she described her relationship with the Holy Spirit. She spoke of Him as if He was a real Person and testified of miracles that occurred in services she held all over the United States. Every Friday, excerpts of those miracle services were broadcast on her program.

"I'll never forget the day my aunt invited me to go with her to a Kathryn Kuhlman miracle rally that was being held in our city. At that point, I didn't know who she was, but I said, 'Sure I'll go.' Amazingly, my parents gave me permission to attend. To have the best seats and be able to see what was happening up front, my aunt suggested that we become a part of Kathryn Kuhlman's choir. So we signed up and began going to choir rehearsals for several days leading up to the event.

"Finally, the day came when we took our seats in the auditorium at the Mabee Center at Oral Roberts University. I remember waiting for the service to begin and watching as the doors opened and the people began flooding into the arena. There were numerous sick folks that came in, including people on stretchers, people in wheel chairs, and even critically ill people with tubes in their arms. By the time the service began, the place was packed to overflowing.

"On cue, we began to sing and lead the people in worship. Then Kathryn Kuhlman came onto the stage, and the moment she did, it felt like a whirlwind of power invaded the auditorium. For the very first time, I felt the presence and power of God like I had never felt Him before.

"'Today I'm going to speak to you for just a few moments,' Kathryn Kuhlman said. Then she spoke for hours, but it only felt like minutes. Then suddenly, she said, 'Somebody in that section over there is being healed.' Everyone listened as she began to speak by the word of knowledge, which is a gift of the Holy Spirit. One by one, she began to point to different sections of the audience and describe in detail the healings that people were experiencing.

"I was astounded as I saw people get out of wheel chairs, rise up off of stretchers, and pull tubes out of their arms. They then lined up near the very front to come on stage and share their testimonies. There were blinded eyes that were opened and deaf ears enabled to hear again. It was as if the Jesus of the gospels stepped onto the stage in front of me and was healing people like He did during the days of His earthly ministry. I was stunned.

"I remember thinking to myself, *Wow, I've been jipped my whole life. I was told the gifts of the Holy Spirit had ceased with the death of the apostles and that God no longer healed like this. Yet here it is happening on the stage right in front of me.*

"I watched as Kathryn Kuhlman partnered with the Holy Spirit, and lives were being powerfully touched and changed. This woman of God had a living, vibrant relationship with the Holy Spirit. And as I sat in my chair looking down on that stage, I said in my heart, *God, You are not a respecter of persons. If You have this kind of relationship with Kathryn Kuhlman by the Holy Spirit, then You can have it with me too!*

"When I left the auditorium that day, I was determined I was going to find this deeper dimension that I was looking for. My resolve put me on the road to personally experience God's power, and on January 11, 1974, I was baptized in and gloriously filled with the Holy Spirit. From that time until now, I've been living in a dynamic relationship with the Holy Spirit."

Vital New Testament Facts About Jesus and the Holy Spirit

No one knew more about the Holy Spirit than Jesus. From His humble birth, nothing He ever did occurred apart from His partnership with the Holy Spirit. Take a few moments to ponder these facts from Scripture:

- Jesus was conceived by the Holy Spirit in the womb of the Virgin Mary. (Matthew 1:18,20; Luke 1:35)

- Jesus' conception in Mary's womb was confirmed by Elisabeth, Mary's cousin, when Elisabeth was temporarily filled with the Holy Spirit. (Luke 1:41-45)

- Jesus' dedication as a baby in the temple was accompanied by supernatural manifestations of the Holy Spirit as Simeon and Anna prophesied over Him.
(Luke 2:25-38)

- Jesus' arrival to Israel as Messiah was announced by John the Baptist, who under the anointing of the Holy Spirit, declared that Jesus was the One who would baptize in the Holy Spirit and with fire.
(Matthew 3:11; Luke 3:16; John 1:33; Acts 11:16)

- Jesus spoke of the baptism in the Holy Spirit and commanded His disciples to stay in Jerusalem until they had received this special endowment of power.
  (Luke 24:49; Acts 1:4,5)

- Jesus was empowered by the Holy Spirit at the Jordan River when He was baptized in water by John the Baptist.
  (Matthew 3:16; Mark 1:10; Luke 3:22; John 1:32)

- Jesus was given the fullness of the Spirit without measure.
  (John 3:34)

- Jesus was led by the Holy Spirit.
  (Matthew 4:1; Mark 1:12; Luke 4:1)

- Jesus returned from the wilderness in the power of the Holy Spirit.
  (Luke 4:14)

- Jesus stated that His ministry was a result of the anointing of the Holy Spirit.
  (Luke 4:18)

- Jesus warned about the danger of blaspheming the Holy Spirit.
  (Matthew 12:31,32; Mark 3:28,29; Luke 12:10)

- Jesus taught extensively about the work and ministry of the Holy Spirit.
  (Matthew 10:20; Mark 13:11; Luke 11:13; 12:12; John 7:39; 14:16,17; 15:26; 16:7-15)

- Jesus proclaimed that we must be born again by the Holy Spirit.
  (John 3:5-8)

- Jesus offered Himself upon the Cross through the sustaining power of the Holy Spirit.
  (Hebrews 9:14)

- Jesus was resurrected from the dead by the power of the Holy Spirit.
  (Romans 8:11)

- Jesus breathed the Holy Spirit into the disciples after His resurrection.
  (John 20:22)

- Jesus instructed the apostles through the ministry of the Holy Spirit.
  (Acts 1:2)

- After Jesus was exalted to the right hand of God, He poured out the Holy Spirit upon the Church on the Day of Pentecost.
  (Acts 2:1-4,33)

From the conception of Jesus' life to His resurrection and ascension into Heaven, we see the Holy Spirit and Jesus inseparably linked. If Jesus needed this kind of ongoing partnership with the Holy Spirit in order to accomplish His divine role in the earth, then we must have this partnership too. Thankfully, Jesus sent the Holy Spirit to give us everything we need to be victorious, successful, faith-filled, overcoming children of God in this world. With the Holy Spirit at our side, we are equipped for every situation in life.

The Heart's Deepest Desire

There are multitudes of Christians who deeply love God but they haven't experienced this deeper dimension of spiritual living. They go to church week after week, serving and giving of themselves tirelessly, yet they wonder why they feel so powerless and empty as Christians. They keep their frustrations to themselves and faithfully keep up the pace, hoping that somehow — someday — things will begin to "click" for them and make sense.

If you've ever been in this condition — or you are experiencing it now — then you know there's nothing more miserable and defeating than being a Christian who is sincerely trying to live the Christian life, but not really knowing the joy and power of the Holy Spirit. The deeper dimension of the Spirit is the same place that Early Believers discovered and the reason they could experience joy — even in the midst of persecution.

Friend, God is calling you onward into a relationship with the Holy Spirit. He beckons you to draw closer and calls you to enter a deeper place with Him. If the cry of your heart is to walk as Jesus walked and to know the power of the Holy Spirit as the disciples did in the book of Acts, then you are in the right place to experience a whole new realm in God!

Jesus wants to gloriously fill you with His Holy Spirit and set you on a path of adventure you will never regret. The Spirit is just waiting for you to surrender and open your heart to Him. In our next lesson, we will begin to look at Jesus' teachings on the Holy Spirit in John 14, 15, and 16.

STUDY QUESTIONS

**Study to shew thyself approved unto God, a workman that needeth
not to be ashamed, rightly dividing the word of truth.**
— 2 Timothy 2:15

1. Rick shared how he reached a point where he began to ask many
   questions about the Holy Spirit. As you begin this study, what questions do *you* have about the Holy Spirit? Take time to write them
   down, and listen for Him to reveal the answers as you work through
   each lesson.

2. Carefully read through the New Testament facts about Jesus and the
   Holy Spirit. Which ones have you not heard that fascinate you most?
   Take some time to look up the related scripture references and allow
   the Holy Spirit to expand your understanding of who He is.

PRACTICAL APPLICATION

**But be ye doers of the word, and not hearers only,
deceiving your own selves.**
— James 1:22

1. What do you believe about the supernatural gifts of the Holy Spirit?
   Do you believe that they are still operating in the Church today? Or
   do you think these gifts ceased with the death of the apostles? On
   what do you base your belief?

2. Are you faithfully reading your Bible, praying, giving financially, and
   going to church regularly, yet it seems like something is missing? Do
   you feel there is more to the Christian life than what you've been
   experiencing? Do you want to begin living in the deeper dimension of
   the Spirit?

3. Seeing how Jesus was inseparably linked with the Holy Spirit His
   entire life, what does this say to you about *your* connection with the
   Holy Spirit?

TOPIC

The Holy Spirit, Our Comforter

SCRIPTURES

1. **John 14:18** — I will not leave you comfortless: I will come to you.
2. **John 14:16** — And I will pray the Father, and he shall give you another Comforter, that he may abide with you for ever.
3. **John 14:8,9** — ...Shew us the Father, and it sufficeth us.... Have I been so long time with you, and yet hast thou not known me, Philip? He that hath seen me hath seen the Father; and how sayest thou then, Shew us the Father?
4. **Hebrews 1:3** (*AMPC*) — He is the sole expression of the glory of God [the Light-being, the out-raying or radiance of the divine], and He is the perfect imprint and very image of [God's] nature....
5. **John 5:19** — ...Verily, verily, I say unto you, The Son can do nothing of himself, but what he seeth the Father do: for what things soever he doeth, these also doeth the Son likewise.

GREEK WORDS

1. "comfortless" — ὀρφανός (*orphanos*): children left without a father or mother; used in a broader sense to describe students who felt abandoned, deserted, forsaken, or discarded by their teacher; either children abandoned by their parents or students forsaken by their teacher; could depict one who feels deprived
2. "pray" — ἐρωτάω (*erotao*): make an earnest request based on a preferred position; a legal word that is generally used in the gospels to describe Jesus' prayer life
3. "another" — ἄλλος (*allos*): another of the same kind; identical; just like the other
4. "another" — ἕτερος (*heteros*): another of a completely different sort
5. "comforter" — παράκλητος (*parakletos*): a compound of παρα (*para*) and καλέω (*kaleo*); the word παρα (*para*) means along and καλέω (*kaleo*) means to call out to someone; one called alongside to urge,

beseech, coach, plead, beg, pray, or train; pictures one who has come closely alongside of another person for the sake of speaking to him, consoling him, coaching him, comforting him, or assisting him with instruction, counsel, or advice; in ancient times, used to depict military leaders who came alongside their troops to urge, exhort, beseech, beg, and plead with them to stand tall and face their battles bravely

SYNOPSIS

Just hours before His crucifixion, Jesus had a very candid conversation with His disciples. Side-by-side, He had been doing life together with them for more than three years, and they were eyewitnesses to Him performing one miracle after another. Now He was reminding them that He would be leaving and going back to the Father in Heaven. Can you imagine how difficult it must have been for the disciples to hear this.

What would life be like without Jesus? Would it ever be the same? Was this the end of their dream? The disciples had grown dependent upon the physical, visible presence of Jesus, something we cannot fully comprehend. Undoubtedly, they were tempted to feel abandoned. Yet in the midst of their fears and tears, Jesus told His disciples, "…I will pray the Father, and he shall give you another Comforter, that he may abide with you for ever" (John 14:16).

What exactly did Jesus mean when He said He would give us "another Comforter"? Who is this Comforter? In what ways is He like Jesus? And what is His job in your life? We will answer these questions and others as we carefully unpack some of Jesus' most important last words found in chapters 14, 15, and 16 of John's gospel.

The emphasis of this lesson:

When Jesus finished His earthly ministry, He prayed to the Father to send us the Holy Spirit. He is exactly like Jesus in every way, and Jesus called Him our Comforter, which means He has been called to walk alongside us all through life — to urge, to beseech, to plead, to beg, to pray, to coach, and to train us.

Jesus Promised Not To Leave Us 'Comfortless'

On the night Jesus was betrayed, the Master had His last supper with the disciples, washed all of their feet, and then shared some very important last words. There were many things Jesus could have talked about such as the formation of the Church, the launching of world missions, and end-time prophecy. However, He chose instead to talk with His disciples about the Person and ministry of the Holy Spirit.

If you think about it, Jesus had been a spiritual father to the disciples. He had walked with them, talked with them, counseled them, and taught them. He was God in the flesh and had showed them how to cast out demons and coached them on how to lay hands on the sick and see them healed. Throughout His ministry, they had become completely reliant upon Him. After telling them that it was the time for Him to return into Heaven (*see* John 13:33), we know from John 14:1 that their hearts were troubled. Jesus addressed their fears by making them this promise: "I will not leave you comfortless..." (John 14:18).

This word "comfortless" is the Greek word *orphanos*, which describes *children left without a father or mother*. It is where we get the word *orphans*. When used in a broader sense, it describes *students who felt abandoned, deserted, forsaken, or discarded by their teacher*. Therefore, it could either picture children abandoned by their parents, students forsaken by their teacher, or simply one who feels deprived. That's how Jesus' disciples were feeling — abandoned and deprived.

We've Been Given the Gift of 'Another Comforter'

What's interesting is that two verses earlier, in John 14:16, Jesus said, "And I will pray the Father, and he shall give you another Comforter, that he may abide with you for ever." Notice the word "pray" here. In Greek, it is the word *erotao*, which is the term most often used to describe Jesus' prayer life in the gospels, and it means *to make an earnest request based on a preferred position*. It's actually a legal term, which means this particular prayer — praying to the Father to send the Comforter — was so crucial that Jesus was going to present His legal case that they must have the help of the Holy Spirit. This case would be so concrete, clear, and unmistakable that the Father would respond to Jesus' strong legal request by sending the Comforter — the Holy Spirit — to help all those who call upon the name of Jesus.

It's also important to notice that Jesus said, "And I will pray the Father, and he shall give you another Comforter..." (John 14:16). The fact that Jesus said the Father "shall *give*" the Holy Spirit means the Spirit is an undeserved gift to the Church that cannot be earned. That is why when Peter stood up to preach God's message of repentance on the Day of Pentecost, he said that the Holy Spirit is a *gift* (*see* Acts 2:38). This gift is from the Father — free and without charge — to everyone who declares Jesus to be the Lord of his or her life. And as a gift, the Holy Spirit is meant to be unwrapped and fully explored.

Jesus described the Holy Spirit as "another Comforter." The word "another" here is very important. There are two Greek words for "another" that Jesus could have used. The one He did *not* use is the Greek word *heteros*, which means *another of a completely different sort*. An example of the use of the word *heteros* is in the word *heterosexual*, which means two *completely different* sexes.

Instead of using the term *heteros* when He talked about sending "another" Comforter, Jesus used the Greek word *allos*, which describes *another of the same kind; identical; just like the other*. Therefore, when Jesus prayed, He asked the Father to send the disciples — and us — another that is *the same kind as Him*. The Comforter is identical to Jesus in every way. In other words, the Holy Spirit thinks exactly like Jesus, sees things exactly like Jesus, talks exactly like Jesus, and operates exactly as Jesus did. So having the Holy Spirit with us is just like having Jesus with us.

Jesus Is the Perfect Imprint of the Father

Interestingly, we see this same concept existing between Jesus and the Father. In John 14:8, "Philip saith unto him, Lord, shew us the Father, and it sufficeth us." In verse 9, Jesus answered Philip and said, "…Have I been so long time with you, and yet hast thou not known me, Philip? He that hath seen me hath seen the Father; and how sayest thou then, Shew us the Father?" This tells us that Jesus and the Father are identical.

Scripture tells us this clearly in Hebrews 1:3 (*AMPC*), which says, "He [Jesus] is the sole expression of the glory of God [the Light-being, the out-raying or radiance of the divine], and He is the perfect imprint and very image of [God's] nature…." Hence, Jesus perfectly reflects the character of the Father in every way. Whatever we see Jesus do in Scripture, is exactly what the Father does. Jesus confirmed this in John 5:19, where He said, "Verily, verily, I say unto you, The Son can do nothing of himself, but what he seeth the Father do: for what things soever he doeth, these also doeth the Son likewise" (John 5:19).

People often ask, "How do I know if it's God's will to heal the sick today?" To answer this question, we just need to look to Jesus and see what He did, because He is the perfect imprint of the Father's nature and will. When Jesus healed someone, it was a demonstration of the Father's will to heal. When Jesus cast out demons and delivered the demon-oppressed, it was a demonstration of the Father's will to set the captive free. Jesus' life — His words, His attitudes, and His actions — during His earthly ministry were perfect expressions of God's will and nature.

When Jesus taught about the Holy Spirit, He took this truth one step further and used the word *allos* to make this point. Remember, the word *allos* means *one of the very same kind*. Just as Jesus perfectly represented the Father, the Holy Spirit perfectly represents Jesus — saying and doing only what Jesus would say and do. He is the perfect representative of Jesus.

Some Christians will say, "I wonder what it was like to do life with Jesus. Wouldn't it have been wonderful to walk with Him, talk with Him, and to hear His voice?" But people who ask these kinds of questions are missing the point of why Jesus sent the Holy Spirit. If you have the Holy Spirit, it's like you still have Jesus. He is "another" — *allos* — Comforter who is just like Jesus in every way.

The Holy Spirit, Our 'Comforter'

It is important to note that Jesus called the Holy Spirit a Comforter *four times* in His final discourse with His disciples. We find this in John 14:16, John 14:26, John 15:26, and John 16:7. This aspect of the Holy Spirit's ministry is vital. Looking once more at John 14:16, Jesus said, "And I will pray the Father, and he shall give you another Comforter, that he may abide with you for ever."

The word "Comforter" here is a translation of the Greek word *parakletos*. It is a compound of the word *para*, which means *alongside*, and the word *kaleo*, which means *to call out to someone*. When these two words are compounded, it describes *one called alongside to urge, beseech, coach, plead, beg, pray, or train*. It pictures one who has come closely alongside another person for the sake of speaking to him, consoling him, coaching him, comforting him, or assisting him with instruction, counsel, or advice. In ancient times, the word *parakletos* was used to depict military leaders who came alongside their troops to urge, exhort, beseech, beg, and plead with them to stand tall and face their battles bravely.

The first use of this word, however, was in a legal sense to denote one who pleaded a case for someone else in a court of law. It was then used to describe a helper or an assistant who was always ready and on standby to help, assist, and strengthen. Furthermore, it denoted a personal counselor or an advisor. Best of all, it pictured a coach who instructs his students and apprentices.

Just as a coach interacts with his pupils, our *parakletos* — our Comforter, the Holy Spirit — draws close to those under His charge to encourage, exhort, urge, counsel, and teach them how to do a better job. In the same way a vocal coach teaches his students how to sing, or a baseball coach instructs his players how to catch, throw, or bat a ball, the Holy Spirit — our coach — stands by us to teach us how to pray for the sick to be healed, to cast out demons, and to be an instrument that manifests God's Kingdom here on earth.

The Holy Spirit's *Position* Is Alongside Us

Looking closer at the word *parakletos* — the Greek word for "Comforter" — we see that the first part of this word is the word *para*, meaning *alongside*. It always carries the idea of *proximity* or *geographical location*. It specifically speaks of being *very close* to or *alongside* someone. The use of this word *para* in these verses in John's gospel carries the idea of coming as close as you can possibly get to someone.

The moment we were born again, the Holy Spirit came to live inside of us. The Bible tells us this in Galatians 4:6 and Ephesians 1:13. Jesus expands on the function of the Holy Spirit in our lives by calling Him the Comforter — *parakletos* — in John 14:16, John 14:26, John 15:26, and John 16:7. This means in our practical, day-to-day relationship, He is like our partner — intimately close by and alongside us. He experientially comes alongside to assist us in the affairs of life and to bring the reality of Jesus Christ into every situation we encounter.

The Holy Spirit's *Mission* Is Specific

The second part of the word *parakletos* — the word for "Comforter" — is the word *kaleo*, which means *to call*. A *kaleo* call always gives *direction, purpose,* and *definition*. God called the Holy Spirit to do something specific in our lives. His Job description is revealed in His name.

(1) The Holy Spirit Remains *Close By Us*

Doctrinally, we understand that the Holy Spirit seals every believer at the moment of salvation (*see* Ephesians 1:13). But when Jesus referred to the Holy Spirit as the "Comforter" in John 14:16, He was speaking of an *experiential* relationship with the Holy Spirit that we can enjoy on a daily basis. His first job is to be with us and close by us through every moment of life.

(2) The Holy Spirit Has a *Calling*

Just as Paul and Peter were called *to be* apostles in the Body of Christ, the Holy Spirit has received a "calling" to do a specific job in this world. He is "called" — *kaleo* — to be "alongside" — *para* — each of us at all times. In that close proximity, He is to provide strength and encouragement — urging us, beseeching us, and telling us to hold our head high, throw our shoulders back, and face our battles bravely. Likewise, He is to empower us to defeat the enemy in every area of our lives.

The Holy Spirit is called to be with you…

- When you are in despair.
- When things are going well.
- When things are not going well.
- When you go to bed at night.
- When you wake up in the morning.
- All throughout your day.

The fact is, the Holy Spirit is with you…

- When you pray.
- When you don't pray.
- When you behave maturely.
- When you experience moments of immaturity.
- When you go to work, church, the grocery store, the beauty salon, the ball game, or the movies.

The Holy Spirit is with you wherever you go, in whatever you do! That is His calling!

(3) The Holy Spirit Has a *Job Assignment*

The Holy Spirit's job is to help us! That help includes convicting us of sin as well as convincing us that we are the righteousness of God in Jesus Christ (*see* 2 Corinthians 5:21). The Spirit's assignment is also to empower us for the work of the ministry. Furthermore, He is to impart spiritual gifts, teach us the Scriptures, and work through us to touch other people. Whatever help we need at any given moment, the Holy Spirit is with us and alongside us to be the help we need — right when we need it! Although He will not do it for us, He will counsel us, coach us, and instruct us on what we need to do in every situation we face.

In our next lesson, we will focus on what it means and what it looks like to be "led" by the Holy Spirit.

STUDY QUESTIONS

Study to shew thyself approved unto God, a workman that needeth not to be ashamed, rightly dividing the word of truth.
— 2 Timothy 2:15

1. The driving motivation of Jesus' life can be clearly seen in John 5:19 and 30. Carefully read these verses and identify Jesus' greatest passion.

2. What is *your* greatest passion? What gets you up every morning and motivates you through each day? In light of the motivating force in Jesus' life, are there any adjustments you need to make in your priorities? If so, what are they?

PRACTICAL APPLICATION

But be ye doers of the word, and not hearers only, deceiving your own selves.
— James 1:22

1. The Holy Spirit is a *gift* from the Father — free and without charge — to everyone who declares Jesus to be the Lord of his or her life. Have you taken time to unwrap the gift of the Holy Spirit? If so, what aspects of His character do you most appreciate? Why?

2. Jesus said the Holy Spirit is our "Comforter" (*parakletos*). This means His job is to draw close to you to encourage, exhort, urge, counsel, and teach you. Are you allowing the Holy Spirit the opportunity to oper-

ate like this in your life? Looking back, describe a pivotal moment in your journey when the Holy Spirit encouraged, counseled, or taught you something you desperately needed to hear.

3. The second part of the word *parakletos* (Comforter) is the word *kaleo*, which means *to call*. Right now the Holy Spirit is walking alongside you, calling out with words of encouragement and counsel. His *kaleo* call always gives *direction, purpose,* and *definition.* In what area of your life do you most need His divine direction or awareness of purpose? Pray and ask Him for the words of wisdom you need.

LESSON 3

TOPIC

Being Led By the Holy Spirit

SCRIPTURES

1. **John 14:16** — And I will pray the Father, and he shall give you another Comforter, that he may abide with you for ever.

2. **Matthew 9:27-30** — And when Jesus departed thence, two blind men followed him, crying, and saying, Thou Son of David, have mercy on us. And when he was come into the house, the blind men came to him: and Jesus saith unto them, Believe ye that I am able to do this? They said unto him, Yea, Lord. Then touched he their eyes, saying, According to your faith be it unto you. And their eyes were opened....

3. **Luke 5:17** — And it came to pass on a certain day, as he was teaching, that there were Pharisees and doctors of the law sitting by, which were come out of every town of Galilee, and Judaea, and Jerusalem: and the power of the Lord was present to heal them.

4. **Romans 8:14** — For as many as are led by the Spirit of God, they are the sons of God.

5. **John 5:19** (*TLB*)— Jesus replied, "The Son can do nothing by himself. He does only what he sees the Father doing, and in the same way.

GREEK WORDS

1. "comforter" — **παράκλητος** (*parakletos*): a compound of **παρα** (*para*) and **καλέω** (*kaleo*); the word **παρα** (*para*) means along and **καλέω** (*kaleo*) means to call out to someone; one called alongside to urge, beseech, coach, plead, beg, pray, or train; pictures one who has come closely alongside of another person for the sake of speaking to him, consoling him, coaching him, comforting him, or assisting him with instruction, counsel, or advice; in ancient times, used to depict military leaders who came alongside their troops to urge, exhort, beseech, beg, and plead with them to stand tall and face their battles bravely

2. "followed" — **ἀκολουθέω** (*akoloutheo*): to follow; to tirelessly accompany someone; to constantly be at the side of an individual; to follow after someone or something in a very determined and purposeful manner

3. "crying" — **κράζω** (*kradzo*): to scream, yell, exclaim, or cry out at the top of one's voice; to shriek; an urgent shout; a loud outburst

4. "saying" — **λέγοντες** (*legontes*): saying, saying, and saying; the tense describes an ongoing action

5. "led" — **ἄγω** (*ago*): to lead: depicted animals led by a rope tied around their necks, who followed wherever their owner led them; the owner would "tug" and "pull" and the animal followed; to be led by a gentle tug or pull; this word forms the root for the Greek word **ἀγών** (*agon*), which describes an intense conflict, such as a struggle in a wrestling match or a struggle of the human will

SYNOPSIS

For many Christians, life seems monotonous and boring. And the reason is because they are not living in the deeper dimension of the Holy Spirit — they are not being led by the Spirit of God. The Bible says, "For as many as are led by the Spirit of God, they are the sons of God" (Romans 8:14). If you are born-again, you are a son or daughter of the Most High and have the right — and privilege — to be led by His Holy Spirit. Make no mistake: when the Spirit is directing your steps, you will experience the adventure of a lifetime!

The emphasis of this lesson:

As a son or daughter of God, you have the right and privilege to be led by the Holy Spirit. Often the Spirit's leading is like a gentle tug or pull in a certain direction. Other times it is an all-out wrestling match in which you must decide to submit your will to His will. The key is learning to become the Holy Spirit's "tagalong" and stay in step with His timing.

A Review of the Meaning of 'Comforter'

In our last lesson, we took a close look at Jesus' words in John 14:16 where He said, "And I will pray the Father, and he shall give you another Comforter, that he may abide with you for ever." We saw that the word "Comforter" is a translation of the Greek word *parakletos*, which is a compound of the word *para*, meaning *alongside*, and the word *kaleo*, which means *to call out to someone*. When these two words are compounded to form the word *parakletos*, it depicts *one called alongside to urge, beseech, coach, plead, beg, pray, or train*. It pictures one who has come closely alongside another person for the sake of speaking to him, consoling him, coaching him, comforting him, or assisting him with instruction, counsel, or advice.

In ancient times, the word *parakletos* was used to depict military leaders who came alongside their troops to urge, exhort, beseech, beg, and plead with them to stand tall and face their battles bravely. And now Jesus used this word to describe the ministry of the Holy Spirit in our lives.

Keep in mind, the first use of the word *parakletos* was in a legal sense, and it described one who pleaded a case for someone else in a court of law, which means the Holy Spirit will plead your case for you. The word *parakletos* was also used to describe a helper or an assistant who was always ready and on standby to help, assist, and strengthen. Furthermore, it depicted a personal counselor or advisor. Best of all, it pictured a trainer or coach who instructs his students and apprentices.

Just as a coach interacts with his pupils, our *parakletos* — our Comforter, the Holy Spirit — draws close to us in order to encourage, exhort, urge, counsel, and teach us how to do a better job. The coach's job is to teach and train, not to perform the actions for us. In the same way a vocal coach teaches his students how to sing or a baseball coach instructs his players how to catch, throw, or hit a ball, the Holy Spirit — our coach — stands by us to teach and train us how to do everything Jesus did to establish God's Kingdom here on earth.

Always remember, you are the apprentice, and in order to fully benefit from the Holy Spirit's coaching and training, you need to open your ears and eyes and be listening and looking for His words of direction. As you do what the Holy Spirit tells you to do, you will always have success.

So often a great deal of what we do is initiated by *us* and not by the Holy Spirit. We proceed with our own "preplanned program" and believe God will automatically bless what we're doing — assuming it's His will because it's a good idea. As a result, we end up missing the leading of the Holy Spirit. No wonder we've had such poor results! Remember, the Holy Spirit sees what we cannot see and knows what we don't know. We must learn to wait until the Holy Spirit speaks about the direction we must go and then obey what He says.

Timing Is Everything

The Bible says there is "…a time to every purpose under heaven" (Ecclesiastes 3:1). This includes a time to minister healing to those who are sick and a time *not* to minister healing. Now, you may say, "Isn't it God's will to heal?" The answer is *yes*! However, sometimes it is not the right moment for a person to be healed. Only the Holy Spirit knows for certain if a person is ready to receive healing. Only He can see the condition of their heart.

For instance, if a person is holding on to unforgiveness and has become bitter toward someone, they are not ready to receive healing. First, he or she must deal with the bitterness in their heart by asking God to forgive them, releasing any offenses they're holding on to, and then blessing that person.

Even Jesus needed to be led by the Holy Spirit in order to know who to pray for to be healed. We see a vivid example of this in the account of the two blind beggars who sought healing from Jesus. The Bible says in Matthew 9:27, "And when Jesus departed thence, two blind men followed him, crying, and saying, Thou Son of David, have mercy on us."

The word "followed" in this verse is the Greek word *akoloutheo*, which means *to follow* and carries the idea of *tirelessly accompanying someone*. It indicates *to constantly be at the side of an individual; to follow after someone or something in a very determined and purposeful manner.* That is what these two blind men were doing. Even though they couldn't see where they were going, these beggars were determined to follow Jesus and cry out until they got His attention.

The word "crying" in Matthew 9:27 is a translation of the Greek word *kradzo*, which means *to scream, yell, exclaim,* or *cry out at the top of one's voice.* It can also mean *to shriek* or describe *an urgent shout* or *a loud outburst.* And the word "saying" is the Greek word *legontes*, and its tense describes an ongoing action. In other words, these two blind men kept on *saying, screaming,* and *yelling.* They were crying out at the top of their lungs trying to get Jesus' attention. Yet, strangely, Jesus just kept walking as if they weren't even there. He didn't stop to heal them!

But that didn't stop these blind beggars. They kept following — screaming, yelling, and crying out saying, "Son of David, have mercy on us!" There is no way Jesus could have missed them because they were yelling so loudly. So why didn't Jesus acknowledge these two blind men, and why didn't He heal them when they first cried out to Him? The answer is, in that moment, *He wasn't led to.* Remember, Jesus said, "…The Son can do nothing by himself. He does only what he sees the Father doing…" (John 5:19 *TLB*). Jesus never initiated a healing. He only did what He felt the Holy Spirit was leading Him to do. Obviously, Jesus didn't feel led to immediately stop and heal these two blind men, or He would have done it.

Matthew goes on to tell us, "And when he [Jesus] was come into the house, the blind men came to him: and Jesus saith unto them, Believe ye that I am able to do this? They said unto him, Yea, Lord. Then touched he their eyes, saying, According to your faith be it unto you. And their eyes were opened…" (Matthew 9:28-30).

Why did Jesus answer them, "According to your faith be it unto you?" Because evidently, in that moment, Jesus didn't sense the healing anointing. It was as if Jesus said, "I don't sense the anointing of the Holy Spirit to heal right now, so you're going to have to receive this one on your own faith! According to your faith, be it done unto you." The good news is that they could use their own faith, and their eyes were opened that day. Nevertheless, Jesus only acted when the Holy Spirit led Him to heal, and because He only acted when He was led, He had a 100-percent success rate.

Are You Following the Leader?

Another example of Jesus being led by the Holy Spirit is found in Luke's gospel. The Bible says, "And it came to pass on a certain day, as he was teaching, that there were Pharisees and doctors of the law sitting by, which were come out of every town of Galilee, and Judaea, and Jerusalem: and the power of the Lord was present to heal them" (Luke 5:17).

In this situation, Jesus clearly sensed the anointing of the Holy Spirit to heal people, and because He felt the anointing of the Spirit, He seized the opportunity to heal a man who was sick with palsy and unable to walk. This miraculous event caused the majority of the witnesses present to praise and glorify God and filled them with the reverential fear of the Lord (*see* Luke 5:20-26).

The key to Jesus' success in ministry is that He learned how to follow the leading of the Holy Spirit — every time. Do you remember playing the game "Follow the Leader" as a child? Whatever the leader said to do, you did it. It's the same way with the Holy Spirit. He is your leader. Whatever He says to do, you need to do it, because He's the leader!

The Spirit's Leading Can Be a Gentle Tug or Pull or an All-Out Wrestling Match

This principle brings us back to the scripture with which we opened our lesson. Romans 8:14 says, "For as many as are led by the Spirit of God, they are the sons of God." What's interesting is that in the original Greek, the sentence structure of this verse is reversed to read, "For as many as by the Spirit are being led, they are the sons of God." It puts the Holy Spirit at the beginning of the verse, and we are placed behind Him — like children who play Follow the Leader!

In order for us to truly be successful in any spiritual endeavor, the Spirit must lead and we must follow. The word "led" in Romans 8:14 is the Greek word *ago*, which means *to lead*, and it depicted animals led by a rope tied around their necks, that followed wherever their owner led them. The owner would "tug" and "pull," and the animals followed. Hence, the word *ago* indicates *being led by a gentle tug or pull.*

It's important to note that the word *ago* forms the root for the Greek word *agon*, which describes *an intense conflict*, such as a struggle in a wrestling match or a struggle of the human will. This word shows that the Holy Spirit desires to lead us, but our human will does not like the idea of being led. Sometimes His leading is so gentle that if we're not looking and listening for it, we'll miss it. Other times the Spirit's leading is like being thrown into a wrestling match, and our soul — which is our mind, will, and emotions — struggles against what the Lord is asking us to do.

In moments like these, we must learn to stay in our place behind the Holy Spirit. We are not to be out front directing the Spirit! Our position is behind Him — following His lead, direction, and guidance. A mature believer has the ability to sense where the Lord is leading and then to follow that leading — even if that leading at the moment means to stay put! We must make it our goal to be the Holy Spirit's "tagalongs." This is truly where our life of adventure begins.

Friend, you have no idea what awaits you as you give the right of way to the Holy Spirit. There are people He will place right in front of you that are in desperate situations, and He will give you the life-giving words to speak in those moments that will give them peace and hope and totally change the direction of their lives. The Holy Spirit is your Heavenly Coach, and you have the right and privilege to be led by Him.

In our remaining lessons, we will focus on ten different things the Holy Spirit does in and through our lives as we look and listen for His leading.

STUDY QUESTIONS

> **Study to shew thyself approved unto God, a workman that needeth not to be ashamed, rightly dividing the word of truth.**
> **— 2 Timothy 2:15**

1. The key to Jesus' success in ministry is that He learned how to follow the leading of the Holy Spirit — every time. Many times the Holy Spirit leads us by His peace. Take time to meditate on this powerful principle in Colossians 3:15 (*AMPC*):

   "And let the peace (soul harmony which comes) from Christ rule (act as umpire continually) in your hearts [deciding and settling with finality all questions that arise in your minds, in that peaceful state] to which as [members of Christ's] one body you were also called [to live]...."

   What is the Holy Spirit showing you from this passage about having His peace with regards to making decisions in your life?

2. When the two blind beggars cried out for Jesus to heal them, Jesus didn't feel led to immediately stop and heal them or He would have. What new insights is the Holy Spirit showing you from this example about God's timing and Him answering your prayers?

3. One of the most important things the Holy Spirit is looking at in each of our lives is *the condition of our heart*. Why do you think the Holy Spirit would wait to answer your prayers until your heart was ready to receive it? Why would He want you to deal with offense and unforgiveness in your heart first and then answer your prayer?

PRACTICAL APPLICATION

> But be ye doers of the word, and not hearers only,
> deceiving your own selves.
> —James 1:22

1. So often a great deal of what we do is initiated by *us* and not by the Holy Spirit. Take a moment to pray: *Lord, is there an area in my life where I'm going with my own "preplanned program"? Have I assumed what I'm doing is Your will and expecting You to automatically bless it? Where have I missed Your leading, Holy Spirit?* Be still and listen. What's God saying to you? Repent of any area where you didn't seek or follow His leading, and do what you need to do to adjust your course.

2. Sometimes the Holy Spirit's leading is a gentle tug or pull. Other times it's like a wrestling match where our soul struggles to submit to what God is asking us to do. Have you ever been in a wrestling match with the Holy Spirit? Are you in one now? Briefly describe the situation and ask the Holy Spirit to show you why your mind, will, and emotions are resistant to His leading.

TOPIC

The Holy Spirit Comforts and Indwells

SCRIPTURES

1. **John 14:16** — And I will pray the Father, and he shall give you another Comforter, that he may abide with you for ever.

2. **John 14:26** — But the Comforter, which is the Holy Ghost, whom the Father will send in my name, he shall teach you all things, and bring all things to your remembrance, whatsoever I have said unto you.

3. **John 15:26** — But when the Comforter is come, whom I will send unto you from the Father, even the Spirit of truth, which proceedeth from the Father, he shall testify of me.

4. **John 16:7** — Nevertheless I tell you the truth; It is expedient for you that I go away: for if I go not away, the Comforter will not come unto you, but if I depart, I will send him unto you.

5. **John 14:17** — Even the Spirit of truth; whom the world cannot receive, because it seeth him not, neither knoweth him: but ye know him; for he dwelleth with you, and shall be in you.

6. **John 20:22** — And when he had said this, he breathed on them, and saith unto them, Receive ye the Holy Ghost.

7. **Genesis 2:7** — And the Lord God formed man of the dust of the ground, and breathed into his nostrils the breath of life; and man became a living soul.

GREEK WORDS

1. "comforter" — **παράκλητος** (*parakletos*): a compound of **παρα** (*para*) and **καλέω** (*kaleo*); the word **παρα** (*para*) means along and **καλέω** (*kaleo*) means to call out to someone; one called alongside to urge, beseech, coach, plead, beg, pray, or train; pictures one who has come closely alongside of another person for the sake of speaking to him, consoling him, coaching him, comforting him, or assisting him with

instruction, counsel, or advice; in ancient times, used to depict military leaders who came alongside their troops to urge, exhort, beseech, beg, and plead with them to stand tall and to face their battles bravely

2. "with" — **παρ'** (*par*): from **παρά** (*para*), alongside

3. "in" — **ἐν** (*en*): in, as inside

4. "breathed" — **ἐμφυσάω** (*emphusao*): to breathe into; to inflate

5. "receive" — **Λάβετε** (*labete*): to take right now; to actively receive

SYNOPSIS

Every week in the Moscow Good News Church — and in churches across the globe — the greatest miracle that could ever happen in a person's life takes place. The moment individuals repent of their sin and surrender their lives to the lordship of Jesus Christ, they are instantaneously born again, and the Holy Spirit moves into their lives as a *permanent resident*.

As a believer, you are the highly decorated temple of the Holy Spirit (*see* 1 Corinthians 6:19). God has called His Spirit to permanently indwell you with the fullness of who He is. And the Spirit's Number 1 job is to serve as the *Comforter* in your life. He is to be alongside you at all times, speaking words of direction, correction, encouragement, counsel, instruction, and advice. He is your personal trainer and your life coach.

The emphasis of this lesson:

First and foremost, the Holy Spirit is your Comforter who is called by God to walk alongside you and speak into your life what you need to hear, when you need to hear it. The moment you were born again, the Holy Spirit came to live inside you and became a permanent resident. He is your Partner for life.

As we begin this fourth lesson, let's first look at an overview of ten specific aspects of the Holy Spirit's work in our lives on a personal level.

Number 1: The Holy Spirit *comforts* us (John 14:16).

Number 2: The Holy Spirit *indwells* us (John 14:17).

Number 3: The Holy Spirit *teaches* us (John 14:26).

Number 4: The Holy Spirit *reminds* us (John 14:26).

Number 5: The Holy Spirit *testifies with* us (John 15:26).

Number 6: The Holy Spirit *convicts* us (John 16:9).

Number 7: The Holy Spirit *convinces* us (John 16:10).

Number 8: The Holy Spirit *guides* us (John 16:13).

Number 9: The Holy Spirit *reveals things* to us (John 16:13).

Number 10: The Holy Spirit *helps us worship* (John 16:14).

When you surrender your life to God, He deposits His Holy Spirit inside of you, and as you partner with Him, He will personally take on these ten tasks in your life. All that is required of you is your cooperation.

NUMBER 1: THE HOLY SPIRIT *COMFORTS* US

Jesus Called the Holy Spirit 'Comforter' Four Times

As we have examined in previous lessons, Jesus used the word "Comforter" four times to describe our partnership with the Holy Spirit. We see this word used in John 14:16, John 14:26, John 15:26, and John 16:7. When a truth is repeated over and over — especially in the short space of three chapters — it is always for the sake of emphasis. Jesus is really trying to drive home this point in the heart of His disciples — and in our hearts.

Look at what Jesus said in these four passages:

- **John 14:16** — "And I will pray the Father, and he shall give you another *Comforter*, that he may abide with you forever."

- **John 14:26** — "But the *Comforter*, which is the Holy Ghost, whom the Father will send in my name, he shall teach you all things, and bring all things to your remembrance, whatsoever I have said unto you."

- **John 15:26** — "But when the *Comforter* is come, whom I will send unto you from the Father, even the Spirit of truth, which proceedeth from the Father, he shall testify of me."

- **John 16:7** — "Nevertheless I tell you the truth; It is expedient for you that I go away: for if I go not away, the *Comforter* will not come unto you; but if I depart, I will send him unto you."

In all four of these verses, the word "Comforter" is a translation of the Greek word *parakletos*. It is a compound of the word *para*, meaning *alongside*, and the word *kaleo*, which means *to call out to someone*. When these two words are compounded to form the word *parakletos*, it depicts *one called alongside to urge, beseech, coach, plead, beg, pray, or train*. It pictures one who has come closely alongside of another person for the sake of speaking to him, consoling him, coaching him, comforting him, or assisting him with instruction, counsel, or advice.

In ancient times, the word *parakletos* — translated in these verses as "Comforter"— was used to depict military leaders who came alongside their troops to urge, exhort, beseech, beg, and plead with them to stand tall and face their battles bravely. It is this particular word — *parakletos* — that Jesus used to describe the ministry of the Holy Spirit in our lives. Just as a teacher is called to teach, a pastor is called to pastor, and a prophet is called to prophesy, the Holy Spirit is explicitly called by God to be alongside us to counsel, console, encourage, coach, and train us. If we will listen, He will download the strategy we need to win in every fight we face.

He Is Our Defense Lawyer. Originally, the earliest use of the word *parakletos* was in a legal sense, and it depicted *one who pleaded a case for someone else in a court of law*. This means if we allow the Holy Spirit to work in our lives, He will come to our defense and serve as our lawyer who pleads our case.

He Is Our Standby. The word *parakletos* was also used to describe *a helper* or *an assistant* who was always ready and on standby to help, assist, and strengthen.

He Is Our Personal Counselor. Furthermore, the word *parakletos* depicted *a personal counselor* or *advisor*.

He Is Our Coach. Of all the meanings of the word *parakletos* (Comforter), one of the best is that it pictures *a trainer* or *coach* who instructs his students and apprentices.

Just as a coach interacts with his students, our *parakletos* — our Comforter, the Holy Spirit — comes close alongside us in order to encourage, exhort, urge, counsel, and teach us what to do in all the issues of our lives. We are His apprentices, and as such we are to do whatever our coach tells us to do. The only way the Holy Spirit's coaching will be a blessing in our lives is if we listen to Him and obey what He says.

In the same way a coach must be trusted and followed, Jesus wanted us to know we can trust the Holy Spirit. This is one of the primary reasons He called the Holy Spirit the "Spirit of Truth" three times in the same three chapters of John's gospel. This was the equivalent of Jesus saying, "I'm sending the Holy Spirit to you as a coach — a coach that you can really trust. He will never mislead or misguide you. Every word He speaks is reliable and true."

As you go through the circumstances of life, the Holy Spirit is right alongside (*para*) to help assist you, defend you, teach you, advise you, strengthen you, and coach you with every step you take.

NUMBER 2: THE HOLY SPIRIT *INDWELLS* US

The Spirit Stays Permanently Inside Every Believer

The second aspect of the Holy Spirit's work in our lives is that Jesus sent Him to *indwell* us. In John 14:17, Jesus said, "Even the Spirit of truth; whom the world cannot receive, because it seeth him not, neither knoweth him: but ye know him; for he dwelleth with you, and shall be *in* you." In this passage, we see a picture of both the *experiential* work and the *residential* work of the Holy Spirit.

The word "with" here is taken from the Greek word *para*, which means *alongside*. So again, Jesus said the Holy Spirit is literally right *alongside* you. And in His very next breath, Jesus said the Spirit is *in* you. The word "in" here is the Greek word *en*, and it means *in, as inside*.

In the Old Testament, the Holy Spirit did not dwell inside anyone. When He came upon people, it was to temporarily empower them for a specific task, assignment, ministry, or service. Even the prophets, priests, and kings of the Old Testament only knew the presence of the Holy Spirit in a temporary way. Once the person finished the job God asked him or her to do, the Holy Spirit would lift off of their life and leave.

In the New Testament, things changed. For the first time in human history, the Holy Spirit began coming INTO people and staying permanently. The disciples of Jesus were the first ones to experience this supernatural miracle.

The Moment the Disciples Got 'Saved'

After Jesus died on the Cross and was raised from the dead, He suddenly materialized in the presence of His disciples who were hiding behind closed doors in an upper room in the city of Jerusalem. Once Jesus showed them the nail scars in His hands and the spear wound in His side, the Bible says, "…He breathed on them, and saith unto them, Receive ye the Holy Ghost" (John 20:22).

Notice the word "breathed" in this verse. It is a translation of the Greek word *emphusao*, which means *to breathe into* or *to inflate*. It's a picture of one taking a balloon, putting it to their lips, and blowing air into it to inflate it. This is what Jesus did to His disciples in the upper room. He breathed *into* them (*emphusao*), and in that divine moment they received the gift of the Holy Spirit.

This same Greek word *emphusao* is also used in Genesis 2:7 of the Septuagint, which is the Greek translation of the Old Testament. This passage describes the moment God breathed into Adam the breath of life. It says, "And the Lord God formed man of the dust of the ground, and breathed into his nostrils the breath of life; and man became a living soul."

The phrase "breathed into" in Genesis 2:7 and the word "breathed" in John 20:22 is the same Greek word — the word *emphusao*. So just as Adam received the breath of God and became a living soul, the disciples received the Holy Spirit when Jesus — who is God in the flesh — breathed on them. The Holy Spirit moved inside of the disciples and became a permanent indweller, and in that very moment they were officially born again.

It's also important to note that when Jesus breathed on His disciples, He said to them, "…Receive ye the Holy Ghost" (John 20:22). The word "receive" is the Greek word *labete*, and it means *to take right now; to actively receive at this very moment*. Jesus told them to receive the Holy Spirit *in that very moment*, and as they did, the Holy Spirit came to permanently live inside human hearts for the first time ever.

This marked a new age when the Holy Spirit would no longer come and go; He would come to permanently dwell in the hearts of all believers. This means your heart is not a hotel that the Holy Spirit comes to visit for a little while and then leaves. Your heart is the Holy Spirit's forever home!

The Holy Spirit Is Your Partner for Life!

Friend, when you got saved, the ultimate miracle was performed inside your heart. When you were born again, you became a dwelling place for the Holy Spirit. God never intended that the Holy Spirit just be your guest. If the Spirit was only a temporary guest, you couldn't develop a close partnership with Him. On the contrary, the Holy Spirit has come to stay as a permanent resident in your heart. He is your Partner for the rest of your life.

This is why you must decide to get serious about cultivating your partnership with the Holy Spirit — starting today! As you cooperate with the Spirit's promptings, He will release His power, His presence, and all of His supernatural works in your life more and more. In our next lesson, we will turn our attention to the Holy Spirit's role of *teaching*, *reminding*, and *testifying*.

STUDY QUESTIONS

> **Study to shew thyself approved unto God, a workman that needeth not to be ashamed, rightly dividing the word of truth.**
> **— 2 Timothy 2:15**

1. In the Old Testament, the Holy Spirit did not dwell inside anyone. When He came upon people, it was to temporarily empower them for a specific task, assignment, ministry, or service. Who can you name from the Old Testament that experienced this type of short-lived anointing? What did God empower them to do?

2. The day Jesus was raised from the dead, He appeared to His disciples in the upper room and breathed on them saying, "…Receive ye the Holy Ghost" (John 20:22). Prior to this lesson, what did you understand about this passage? Had you even heard of it? What new insights did you learn about the disciples and this divine moment in history?

3. As your Comforter, the Holy Spirit serves as your *personal counselor*. Write out and commit to memory the powerful promise God made to you in Psalm 32:8 about receiving His counsel. (Also consider Psalm 25:12; Isaiah 30:21; Jeremiah 33:2,3.)

4. According to James 1:5-7, what do you need to do to receive godly wisdom to handle life's circumstances and situations?

PRACTICAL APPLICATION

But be ye doers of the word, and not hearers only,
deceiving your own selves.
— James 1:22

1. Can you remember the day that the Holy Spirit came and made Himself a permanent resident inside your heart? What was that day like?

2. Four times Jesus called the Holy Spirit our "Comforter" — the Greek word *parakletos* — a word with deep, multi-faceted meaning. In what specific ways have you personally experienced the Holy Spirit functioning as the Comforter in your life?

3. Stop and think: *What kind of home am I for the Holy Spirit? Do I make Him feel welcome every day or do I barely acknowledge His presence? What am I doing to get to know Him better, and how am I developing a closer friendship and partnership with Him?*

LESSON 5

TOPIC

The Holy Spirit Teaches, Reminds, and Testifies

SCRIPTURES

1. **John 14:26** — But the Comforter, which is the Holy Ghost, whom the Father will send in my name, he shall teach you all things, and bring all things to your remembrance, whatsoever I have said unto you.

2. **John 16:13,15** — ...He shall not speak of himself; but whatsoever he shall hear, that shall he speak...He shall take of mine, and shall show it unto you.

3. **1 Corinthians 2:9,10** — ...Eye hath not seen, nor ear heard, neither have entered into the heart of man, the things which God hath prepared for them that love him. But God hath revealed them unto us

by his Spirit: for the Spirit searcheth all things, yea, the deep things of God.

4. **1 Corinthians 2:12** — Now we have received, not the spirit of the world, but the spirit which is of God; that we might know the things that are freely given to us of God.

5. **1 John 2:20** — But ye have an unction from the Holy One, and ye know all things.

6. **John 15:26** — But when the Comforter is come, whom I will send unto you from the Father, even the Spirit of truth, which proceedeth from the Father, he shall testify of me.

7. **Acts 1:8** — But ye shall receive power, after that the Holy Ghost is come upon you: and ye shall be witnesses unto me both in Jerusalem, and in all of Judaea, and in Samaria, and unto the uttermost part of the earth.

GREEK WORDS

1. "teach" — **διδάσκω** (*didasko*): to teach, to instruct, or to prescribe; this word was primarily used to describe the relationship between a teacher and a pupil or a master and apprentice; what is taught may be not only knowledge, opinions, or facts but also artistic and technical skills, all of which are to be systematically and thoroughly acquired by the learner through the activity of a teacher

2. "revealed" — **ἀποκάλυψις** (*apokalupsis*): refers to something that has been veiled or hidden, but then becomes clear and visible to the mind or eye; an unveiling; a sudden revealing; to uncover; something that is veiled or hidden but suddenly the veil is removed and what was hidden now comes into plain view; because the veil has been removed what is behind the veil is no longer concealed or hidden from view

3. "by his Spirit" — **διὰ τοῦ Πνεύματος** (*dia tou Pneumatos*): by the Spirit; through the Spirit; by the instrumentality of the Spirit

4. "searches" — **ἐρευνάω** (*ereunao*): to investigate, to examine, or to sift; pictures one who goes through stacks of material looking for something; to carefully investigate, examine, and sift through the materials in one's search for what he needs

5. "deep" — **βάθος** (*bathos*): the deepest parts of the sea; denotes deep thoughts, deep spiritual truths, or deeply laid plans

6. "know" — **οἶδα** (*oida*): to see, perceive, understand, or comprehend

7. "testify" — **μάρτυς** (*martus*): to give a first-hand testimony in a court of law; first-hand knowledge; a factual and dependable account
8. "witnesses" — **μάρτυς** (*martus*): to give a first-hand testimony in a court of law; first-hand knowledge; a factual and dependable account

SYNOPSIS

In our last lesson we learned about the first two aspects of the work of the Holy Spirit in our lives as believers. First, Jesus said the Spirit is our "Comforter" — our *parakletos* — who comes close alongside us in order to encourage, exhort, urge, counsel, and teach us what to do in all the matters of our lives. He is our supernatural life coach that instructs and trains us in everything that concerns us.

Secondly, the Holy Spirit *indwells* us. From the day that Jesus Christ was raised back to life until now, the Holy Spirit has been birthing people into the Kingdom of God and taking up permanent residency inside their lives. No longer is the Spirit a temporary guest that comes and goes as He did in the Old Testament times. As born-again children of God, we have become the temple of the Holy Spirit! As a believer, you are His forever home!

What else does the Holy Spirit desire to do in your life? Jesus said the Spirit wants to teach you all things, remind you of all things, and testify to you and through you about who Jesus is.

The emphasis of this lesson:

The Holy Spirit has been given to us to teach us all things — He's the Master and we are His pupils. Not only does He reveal to us the deep things of God, He also reminds us of what the Word of God says, providing us with the right verse at the right time. Moreover, the Holy Spirit also testifies to us about Jesus and testifies through us to those who are lost.

Ten Aspects of the Holy Spirit's Work

There are so many wonderful things the Holy Spirit — the third Person of the trinity — wants to do in your life, and Jesus told us all about them John's gospel. Here is a quick overview of ten specific roles the Holy Spirit is ready, willing, and able to fill in your life and the life of every believer:

Number 1: The Holy Spirit *comforts* us (John 14:16).

Number 2: The Holy Spirit *indwells* us (John 14:17).

Number 3: The Holy Spirit *teaches* us (John 14:26).

Number 4: The Holy Spirit *reminds* us (John 14:26).

Number 5: The Holy Spirit *testifies to* us and *through* us (John 15:26).

Number 6: The Holy Spirit *convicts* us (John 16:9).

Number 7: The Holy Spirit *convinces* us (John 16:10).

Number 8: The Holy Spirit *guides* us (John 16:13).

Number 9: The Holy Spirit *reveals things* to us (John 16:13).

Number 10: The Holy Spirit *helps us worship* (John 16:14).

Friend, the Bible says, "… You have everything when you have Christ, and you are filled with God through your union with Christ…" (Colossians 2:10 *TLB*). The moment you were saved, the Spirit of Christ — the Holy Spirit — became a permanent indweller inside of you! And as you partner with Him, He will personally go to work in your life. All that is required of you is your cooperation.

NUMBER 3: THE HOLY SPIRIT *TEACHES* US

He Is the Master, We are the Students

Turning our attention once more to John 14:26, Jesus said, "But the Comforter, which is the Holy Ghost, whom the Father will send in my name, he shall teach you all things…." So in addition to the Holy Spirit being our Comforter, He is also our *Teacher*. The word "teach" in this verse is a form of the Greek word *didasko*, which means *to teach, to instruct*, or *to prescribe*. This word was primarily used to describe the relationship between a teacher and a pupil or a master and an apprentice, which indicates that the Holy Spirit was sent to be our Master and we are His apprentice.

What He teaches us may be not only knowledge, opinions, or facts but also artistic and technical skills, all of which are to be systematically and thoroughly acquired by the learner through the activity of a teacher. So the Holy Spirit doesn't just teach us information — He also teaches us the practical skills we need to do the work of the ministry and fulfill our particular calling.

The Spirit's Chief Role Is To Speak on Behalf of Jesus

God has provided the Church with many human teachers who are helpful in equipping us with the truth we need to grow in the things of God. But first and foremost, He has given each of us the Holy Spirit as the ultimate Teacher who will never fail us or lead us astray! Jesus said He is the Spirit of Truth and "...He shall not speak of himself; but whatsoever he shall hear, that shall he speak...He shall take of mine, and shall show it unto you" (John 16:13,15).

The Holy Spirit's chief role as a Teacher is to speak for Jesus Christ. The Spirit brings us the mind of Christ and the will of God. This is why Paul wrote, "...Eye hath not seen, nor ear heard, neither have entered into the heart of man, the things which God hath prepared for them that love him" (1 Corinthians 2:9). Now some Christians see this verse and say that there are just some things about God we can't know or understand. But if they will read further into the next verse, Paul continued by saying, "But God hath revealed them unto us by his Spirit: for the Spirit searcheth all things, yea, the deep things of God" (1 Corinthians 2:10).

By ourselves, we lack the ability to understand the deep things of God. We could never dream, imagine, or conjure up the things God has prepared for us who love Him. Therefore, to help us come to know and experience these blessings, God has given us His amazing Holy Spirit to reveal these things to us.

The word "revealed" in First Corinthians 2:10 is the Greek word *apokalupsis*, which refers to *something that has been veiled or hidden, but then suddenly becomes clear and visible to the mind or eye*. It is an *unveiling* or a *sudden revealing*. It pictures something that is veiled or hidden, but suddenly the veil is removed and what was hidden now comes into plain view. Because the veil has been removed, what is behind the veil is no longer concealed or hidden from view. Hence, the Holy Spirit has been given to us to reveal what our eyes previously could not see, our ears could not hear, and our hearts could not understand.

The Bible says this revealing is done "by his Spirit." This three-word phrase in Greek is *dia tou Pneumatos*, and it means *by the Spirit; through the*

Spirit; or *by the instrumentality of the Spirit.* It is the Holy Spirit who "…searcheth all things, yea, the deep things of God" (1 Corinthians 2:10).

The Spirit 'Searches' Out the Deep Truths and Thoughts of God

The word "searches" is a form of the Greek word *ereunao*, which means *to investigate, to examine,* or *to sift.* It pictures one who goes through stacks of information and material looking for something. This word "searches" means *to carefully investigate, examine, and sift through the materials in one's search for what he needs.* Specifically, the Holy Spirit is thoroughly searching out the "deep things of God."

This word "deep" is derived from the Greek term *bathos*, which is the word used to describe *the deepest parts of the sea.* It denotes *deep thoughts, deep spiritual truths,* or *deeply laid plans.* This is what the Holy Spirit specializes in searching out — the very deepest truths and thoughts of God. He lovingly pulls back the curtain so we can see these things very clearly.

The apostle Paul goes on to say in First Corinthians 2:12, "Now we have received, not the spirit of the world, but the spirit which is of God; that we might know the things that are freely given to us of God." Again, the Holy Spirit is our Teacher, and He helps us know all things. The word "know" here in this verse is the Greek word *oida*, and it means *to see, to perceive, to understand,* or *to comprehend.* If we will submit to the Holy Spirit and listen to Him, He will remove the veil of obscurity and confusion and open our eyes to see amazing truths in the Word of God.

The apostle John wrote about this in his first epistle saying, "But ye have an unction from the Holy One, and ye know all things" (1 John 2:20). The Holy Spirit is your Teacher! But He can only teach you IF you have an experiential partnership with Him!

NUMBER 4: THE HOLY SPIRIT *REMINDS* US

The Holy Spirit Illuminated the Minds of the Apostles

There is something else Jesus said the Holy Spirit does for us in John 14:26. Not only is He our "Comforter" and our "Teacher," Jesus said the Holy Spirit will "…bring all things to your remembrance, whatsoever I have said unto you." If you've ever wondered how the disciples remembered all the things Jesus taught them, now you know how. It was the Holy Spirit who brought to their remembrance all the truths Jesus spoke in the time He was with them.

In the same way, the Holy Spirit reminded all four of the gospel writers of all the intricate details of Jesus' life and ministry. The Spirit supernaturally illuminated their minds and brought back to their remembrance the facts of His birth, His miracles, His interaction with people, as well as His death, burial, and glorious resurrection from the grave! And the very same Holy Spirit has been given to *you* to illuminate your mind and remind you of all things!

Learn To Lean on the Spirit To Recall God's Word

When our partnership with the Holy Spirit is strong, we can lean upon Him to remind us of what the Word of God says. We might be in the midst of a situation in which we don't know what to do. Thankfully, the Holy Spirit is always alongside us to reach into the Word of God, illuminate the exact verse or truth we need, and put us in remembrance of it at just the right moment.

Perhaps this responsibility of the Holy Spirit is most vividly illustrated in parts of the world where the Bible is illegal. For example, communist governments have strictly forbidden the printing and distribution of the Word of God for years, yet underground believers in those nations know the Scripture very well and can quote it word for word. In the former Soviet Union, the Bible had been forbidden there for more than 70 years, yet many believers there could quote it and remember it better than people in free countries who have several Bibles in their houses and the opportunity to read them every morning and every night!

There is only one explanation for this amazing retention of Scripture in believers' hearts in closed countries — the Holy Spirit. He is still doing exactly what Jesus said He would do — putting believers in remembrance of the Word of God. That's one of the Holy Spirit's most valuable responsibilities as our Partner in this world.

First *to You,* Then *Through You*

In John 15:26, Jesus said, "But when the Comforter is come, whom I will send to you from the Father, even the Spirit of truth, which proceedeth from the Father, he shall testify of me." This passage reveals the fifth aspect of the Holy Spirit's work in our lives, and that is to *testify* of Jesus — both *to* us and *through* us.

In Greek, the word "testify" is the word *martus,* and it means *to give a first-hand testimony in a court of law.* It depicts one speaking *first-hand knowledge*; *a factual and dependable account.* As believers, the Holy Spirit gives us reliable, first-hand testimony of who Jesus is and what He did. The fact is, the Holy Spirit loves to talk about Jesus! So first He testifies *to you* about Jesus! Second, He will testify *through you* to people who are lost.

This practice of "testifying to others about Jesus" is what we often call witnessing. For many, the thought of witnessing is energizing and exciting. For others, it brings feelings of anxiety and dread. Images of going door to door and attempting to talk to total strangers about Jesus can be unnerving. In many churches, the pastor has to practically beg people to participate in visitation and evangelism programs.

Why do so many Christians detest and struggle with sharing their faith? Because they are not relying upon the power and Person of the Holy Spirit. When you testify without the Holy Spirit's participation, it is a dead work of the flesh that doesn't produce much fruit. The key to success-ful witnessing is to always invite the supernatural power and partnership of the Holy Spirit.

Jesus said the Holy Spirit will give you the words about Him you need to share with others. It will be a factual and dependable account of Jesus that is anointed by the Holy Spirit. As you abide in partnership with Him, you can trust Him to faithfully fill your mind and mouth with life-changing words of truth!

The Difference Between Before and After Pentecost

Jesus told the disciples to stay in Jerusalem to receive power and part-nership with the Holy Spirit. Then in Acts 1:8 He added, "But ye shall receive power, after that the Holy Ghost is come upon you: and ye shall be witnesses unto me both in Jerusalem, and in all of Judea, and in Samaria, and unto the uttermost part of the earth."

Interestingly, the word "witnesses" in this verse is again the Greek word *martus* — the same word translated as "testify" in John 15:26. It describes *a first-hand testimony in a court of law*, *first-hand knowledge*; or *a factual and dependable account*. Jesus told His disciples they would be witnesses "after" the Holy Spirit came upon them.

To be able to testify powerfully requires power. Before the Day of Pentecost, the disciples were hiding behind closed doors for fear of the Jews. But after the Holy Spirit came upon them in Acts 2, they blasted out of their hiding place and hit the streets of Jerusalem — yielded to the Spirit and preaching with His anointing. Filled to overflowing with the power of the Spirit, Peter stood and boldly proclaimed:

> **Ye men of Israel, hear these words; Jesus of Nazareth, a man approved by God among you by miracles and wonders and signs, which God did by him in the midst of you....Ye have taken, and by wicked hands have crucified and slain: whom God hath raised up, having loosed the pains of death.... Therefore being by the right hand of God exalted... (Acts 2:22-24,33).**

This was a supernatural proclamation and supernatural evangelism at its best!

Let Witnessing Become a Supernatural Event!

Please understand, there is nothing wrong with preplanned evangelism, door-to-door visitation, or evangelism programs that teach us the basics of witnessing. However, when those programs replace the presence and power of the Holy Spirit, it negates what God intended witnessing to be and is not fruitful. True biblical witnessing involves yielding to the leading of the Holy Spirit and receiving His power to eternally impact a life with the truth of Jesus Christ. He holds the key to unlock every human heart and knows how to speak a personalized message of truth each person can receive and believe.

To be clear: Witnessing that occurs separate from the power of the Holy Spirit feels like a dry, dead, non-gratifying religious work. On the contrary, when the Holy Spirit partners with us and we partner with Him, He will speak through us to others about Jesus, and it won't be dry or dead. It will be energizing and full of life! So why reduce testifying to a mere program? Let it become a supernatural event!

Remember, the Holy Spirit was sent to testify of Jesus, and no one knows how to testify better than He does! If you are afraid to witness, then open your heart to the partnership of the Spirit and let *Him* take responsibility for testifying about Jesus *through* you. Make every effort to submit to the Holy Spirit and become His apprentice. Look for and listen to His voice in your life. Obey Him explicitly in whatever He tells you to do, and your life will take on a whole new meaning.

In our next lesson, we will continue our study by looking at how the Holy Spirit works to convict and convince us of certain things in our lives.

STUDY QUESTIONS

> **Study to shew thyself approved unto God, a workman that needeth not to be ashamed, rightly dividing the word of truth.**
> **— 2 Timothy 2:15**

1. One of the greatest roles the Holy Spirit plays in your life is that He is your *Master Teacher*. Name one of the most valuable things the Holy Spirit has taught you about *God*, about *yourself*, and about *others*.

2. By ourselves, we lack the ability to understand the deep things of God. But God has given us the Holy Spirit to reveal these truths to us. If you want to really understand Scripture, invite the author of Scripture — the Holy Spirit — to reveal its meaning to you. He will do for you what Jesus did for the two disciples on the road to Emmaus. Check out their story in Luke 24:13-35.

3. If you're afraid to witness, then open your heart to the power and partnership of the Holy Spirit and let *Him* take responsibility for testifying about Jesus through you. What can you count on the Holy Spirit doing? Consider Jesus' words in Luke 12:11,12 (*also* Matthew 10:19,20).

PRACTICAL APPLICATION

> **But be ye doers of the word, and not hearers only, deceiving your own selves.**
> **— James 1:22**

1. Have you ever seen images you wish you could forget? Or remembered song lyrics you wish you had never heard? If the enemy can remind you of his trash, then the Holy Spirit — who is the Greater One — can certainly remind you of the truth of God's Word! If you want to begin remembering the verses you read and study, pray this prayer: *Holy Spirit, thank You for being my personal Teacher who permanently lives in me. I ask You to help me hide God's Word in my heart and give me total recall of it — chapter and verse. Nothing is too difficult for You! I praise You for giving me this divine ability to bring You glory. In Jesus' name. Amen!*

2. Have you ever participated in witnessing door to door like Rick talked about? If so, how would you describe the experience? If not, what kind of witnessing or evangelism efforts have you participated in?

3. Recall a time when you were able to effortlessly tell someone about Jesus and it was an overall good experience. Were you relying on the supernatural power and partnership of the Holy Spirit? What did you enjoy most and what was most encouraging about the experience?

LESSON 6

TOPIC

The Holy Spirit Convicts and Convinces

SCRIPTURES

1. **John 16:8** — And when he is come, he will reprove the world of sin, and of righteousness....

2. **2 Corinthians 4:4** — In whom the god of this world hath blinded the minds of them which believe not lest the light of the glorious gospel of Christ, who is the image of God, should shine unto them.

3. **John 6:44** — No man can come unto me, except the Father which hath sent me draw him....

4. **Ephesians 5:14** — Wherefore he saith, Awake thou that sleepest, and arise from the dead, and Christ shall give thee light.

5. **2 Corinthians 5:21** — For he hath made him to be sin for us, who knew no sin; that we might be made the righteousness of God in him.

GREEK WORDS

1. "reprove" — ἐλέγχω (*elegcho*): to expose, to convict, or to cross-examine for the purpose of conviction, as when convicting a lawbreaker in a court of law; the image of a lawyer who brings forth evidence that is indisputable and undeniable, so that the accused person's actions are irrefutably brought to light and, as a result, the offender is exposed and convicted; used in a positive sense to convince someone of something; pictures a lawyer who works diligently to convince people of a new way of thinking or a new way of seeing things; in this case, they weren't trying to convict someone, they were working to convince

2. "blinded" — τυφλόω (*tuphloo*): blind; it doesn't just depict a person who is unable to see, but one who has been intentionally blinded by someone else; one whose eyes have been deliberately removed so that he is blinded; this individual hasn't just lost his sight, he has no eyes with which to see

SYNOPSIS

One of the greatest ways to know for sure that God is at work in the life of an unbeliever is seeing that he or she is being *convicted of sin*. Jesus said when the Holy Spirit comes, "…He will reprove the world of sin…" (John 16:8). Likewise, Jesus also said the Holy Spirit would work in the lives of believers, *convincing* them that they are righteous in Him.

Just as unbelievers need the convicting power of the Holy Spirit to know that they are sinners, believers need the convincing power to know that they are righteous. These are two vital aspects of the work of the Holy Spirit we will explore in this lesson.

The emphasis of this lesson:

The first and foremost function of the Holy Spirit is to convict sinners of their sin and reveal to them their true spiritual condition. Amazingly, it is the same Spirit that moves on the minds and hearts of all believers to convince us that we are the righteousness of God in Christ Jesus.

A Review of the Ten Aspects of the Holy Spirit's Work

Thus far, we have explored five specific functions of the Holy Spirit in the life of every believer. As a permanent resident in our hearts, He desires to be actively involved in each area of our lives. In John's gospel, Jesus described ten specific things that the Holy Spirit longs to do in your life:

Number 1: The Holy Spirit *comforts* us (John 14:16).

Number 2: The Holy Spirit *indwells* us (John 14:17).

Number 3: The Holy Spirit *teaches* us (John 14:26).

Number 4: The Holy Spirit *reminds* us of things (John 14:26).

Number 5: The Holy Spirit *testifies to* us and *through* us (John 15:26).

Number 6: The Holy Spirit *convicts* us (John 16:9).

Number 7: The Holy Spirit *convinces* us (John 16:10).

Number 8: The Holy Spirit *guides* us (John 16:13).

Number 9: The Holy Spirit *reveals things* to us (John 16:13).

Number 10: The Holy Spirit *helps us worship* (John 16:14).

No one knows you like the Holy Spirit. He is able to go where no man or woman can go — inside your heart and mind! Only the Spirit of God can penetrate deep inside your soul and spirit and identify the root issues you're dealing with and present you the fool-proof solution to your situation. With that kind of divine power and accuracy, don't you think it's in your best interest to begin to fully know the Holy Spirit?

NUMBER 6: THE HOLY SPIRIT *CONVICTS* US

The Eyes and Ears of Sinners Are Supernaturally Opened

Do you remember when you were a child and you did something wrong, but you thought no one was watching? Then you got caught. You were unmistakably guilty and couldn't escape facing the facts. Can you recall what it was like to feel so exposed? That's what sinners feel the first time the Holy Spirit convicts them of sin.

In John 16:8, Jesus said when the Holy Spirit comes, "…He will reprove the world of sin…." The word "reprove" in this verse is a translation of the Greek word *elegcho*, which means *to expose, to convict*, or *to cross-examine for the purpose of conviction, as when convicting a lawbreaker in a court of law*. It is the image of a lawyer who brings forth evidence that is indisputable and undeniable, so that the accused person's actions are irrefutably brought to light and, as a result, the offender is exposed and convicted.

The word *elegcho* — translated here as "reprove" — was also used in a positive sense, meaning to *convince* someone of something, which we will see in a few moments. But in the case of sinners, it describes the convicting power of the Holy Spirit. The Word of God suddenly becomes so razor sharp that it penetrates a sinner's soul until he feels as if he has been cross-examined on a witness stand. Finally, the verdict is announced and the sinner knows he is guilty.

It's amazing to see how sinners can live for years on end with no conviction of sin whatsoever. They are comfortable in their ungodly behavior and undisturbed by their spiritual condition. Ephesians 4:18 and 19 says they are "alienated from the life of God" and that sin makes them *hardhearted*, *spiritually blind*, and *past feeling*. Moreover, the Bible says they are spiritually dead, insensitive, and non-responsive to God (*see* Ephesians 2:1). This is why unsaved people do the same wrong things over and over again.

But that state of hardheartedness changes instantly when the Holy Spirit touches the human soul and exposes its sinful condition. The Spirit supernaturally enables sinners to hear the Word of God in a brand-new way for the first time, and they are awakened to see their true spiritual condition, feeling exposed, naked, and confronted. When the Holy Spirit goes to work, He arouses within sinners a realization that they are lost and are heading to hell unless they repent and accept the finished work of Jesus Christ. Jesus said the Holy Spirit would reprove people of sin in this way in order to bring them to the saving knowledge of Jesus Christ.

The Holy Spirit Awakens Us to Our Sinfulness and Our Need for Christ

According to Scripture, the whole world stands guilty of sin before God (*see* Romans 3:19). However, the whole world does not realize it is guilty before God, and Second Corinthians 4:4 tells us why. Here Paul stated, "…The god of this world hath blinded the minds of them which believe not lest the light of the glorious gospel of Christ, who is the image of God, should shine unto them."

The word "blinded" here is the Greek word *tuphloo*, and while it means *to be blind*, it doesn't just depict a person who is unable to see, but *one who has been intentionally blinded by someone else*. It is one whose eyes have been deliberately removed so that he is blinded. This individual hasn't just lost his sight; he has no eyes with which to see.

By using this word, God is telling us that without the convicting work of the Holy Spirit to expose our sinful condition, no one can really see it. This is why it can be frustrating to share Christ with family and friends. You share, talk, and plead with them to receive Christ, yet it seems they just can't see what you are saying. They have no spiritual eyes to see or spiritual ears to hear the truth.

This is why Jesus said, "...No man can come unto me, except the Father which hath sent me draw him..." (John 6:44). This dead spiritual state requires a special, supernatural work of the Holy Spirit to rouse the human consciousness to the reality of its sinful condition. Think about it. How can you make a blind man see? How do you show a spiritually blind man spiritual truths? Only the Holy Spirit can touch our souls — awaken us to our sinfulness — and beckon us to give our lives to Christ.

At that divine moment, God speaks to our spirits and says, "...Awake thou that sleepest, and arise from the dead, and Christ shall give thee light" (Ephesians 5:14). There is no greater miracle than this! This convicting work of the Holy Spirit is the first thing He ever does in our lives — and it is just the beginning!

NUMBER 7: THE HOLY SPIRIT *CONVINCES* US

A New Way of Thinking and Seeing Things

In addition to convicting unbelievers of sin, Jesus said the Holy Spirit will also reprove believers of *righteousness* (*see* John 16:8). As we noted, the word "reprove" is a translation of the Greek word *elegcho*, which means *to expose, to convict*, or *to cross-examine for the purpose of conviction, as when convicting a lawbreaker in a court of law*. It is the image of a lawyer who brings forth evidence that is indisputable and undeniable, so that the accused person's actions are irrefutably brought to light and, as a result, the offender is exposed and convicted.

With regards to righteousness, the word *elegcho* — translated here as "reprove" — is used in a positive sense, and it means *to convince someone of something*. It pictures a lawyer who works diligently to convince people of a new way of thinking or a new way of seeing things. In this case, they aren't trying to convict someone of a crime; they are working to convince someone of something good. This depicts the convincing ministry of the Holy Spirit. Specifically, Jesus said the Spirit will come to convince us of *righteousness*.

If there is any subject in Scripture that Christians will argue about, it is righteousness. Most believers are so conscious of their old, sinful nature that they can't embrace the truth that God has made them righteous. When they are told they are righteous, they'll tell you how bad they are. It takes a special work of the Holy Spirit to convince us of our righteousness.

Are You Insulting God's Great Work?

Think about it. Have you ever complimented someone and they rejected it? For instance, you told a friend she looks as if she lost weight, and she responded, "Oh, no. I'm just as fat and ugly as ever. Actually, I've never looked worse." Though unintentional, this is a rude way to respond to a compliment. In fact, it is the equivalent of throwing the compliment back in your face. It would be far more polite to be gracious and say, "Thank you. I'm so grateful you think that, and I appreciate you telling me I look better."

The truth is, many Christians do this to God all the time! The Bible clearly states, "For he [God] hath made him [Jesus] to be sin for us, who knew no sin; that we might be made the righteousness of God in him" (2 Corinthians 5:21). In Christ, we are righteous. But when we argue with God and tell Him how terrible we are, it's like insulting His great work in our lives!

It takes the supernatural work of the Holy Spirit to convince us of righteousness. Otherwise when God says, "You're My child. I have made you righteous. You are beautiful to Me," your mind will reply, "It's not so! I'm unworthy. I'm unholy. I'm so pitiful!" Again, this is like throwing the "compliment" back in God's face!

Awaken to the Fact That You Are Righteous in Christ!

Ephesians 2:10 says, "...We are his workmanship, created in Christ Jesus unto good works...." In the Greek, this literally means we are God's *masterpiece*. This is a powerful truth that only the Holy Spirit can take and transform from mere head knowledge into a heart revelation.

Just as the Spirit must *convict* the sinner of his lost condition, He must *convince* the believer of his new right standing with God. This realization is as supernatural as when a lost man realizes he is lost. Only this time, the Holy Spirit is awakening us to the fact that we are righteous!

If you're struggling to believe you are the righteousness of God in Christ Jesus, take time each day to meditate on Second Corinthians 5:21. Personalize the verse and post it in highly visible places around your house. Listen to teaching on righteousness. Eventually, the convincing power of the Holy Spirit will kick into high gear, and your mind will begin to grasp this powerfully important revelation and it will become rooted in your heart.

When you know that Jesus Christ *made* you righteous, you pray with great boldness and authority! Once your spiritual eyes have been opened and you truly understand that God made you to be righteous, you will never again throw this truth back in His face and argue with Him. Instead, you can embrace your new right standing with Him and escape the prison of perpetual guilt, shame, and condemnation.

In our next lesson, we will focus on the Holy Spirit's work as our supernatural Guide.

STUDY QUESTIONS

**Study to shew thyself approved unto God, a workman that needeth
not to be ashamed, rightly dividing the word of truth.
— 2 Timothy 2:15**

1. What did the apostle Paul say about the condition of the entire human race in Romans 3:10-12 (a reiteration of what David wrote in Psalm 14:1-3)? How does this help you better see and appreciate the convicting work of the Holy Spirit that led you to salvation?

2. Second Corinthians 5:21 says, "For he [God] hath made him [Jesus] to be sin for us, who knew no sin; that we might be made the righteousness of God in him." How do you respond when you hear this truth — that you are righteous in Christ?

3. If you struggle to believe that you're the righteousness of God in Christ, take time every day to meditate on and declare out loud 2 Corinthians 5:21 and ask the Holy Spirit to supernaturally convince you of your righteousness. And while you're at it, reflect on and declare these personalized truths that crush the enemy's attacks of condemnation.

   - "There is therefore now no condemnation [for me] who is in Christ Jesus, who does not walk according to the flesh, but according to the Spirit" (Romans 8:1 *NKJV*).

   - "For God did not send His Son [to me] to condemn [me], but that [I] through Him might be saved. [I] who believe in Him [Jesus] am not condemned..." (John 3:17,18 *NKJV*).

   - "It is the Sovereign Lord who helps me. Who will condemn me? They will all wear out like a garment; the moths will eat them up" (Isaiah 50:9 *NIV*).

PRACTICAL APPLICATION

**But be ye doers of the word, and not hearers only,
deceiving your own selves.
— James 1:22**

1. Can you remember the first time the Holy Spirit brought conviction to your soul, supernaturally revealing to you your true spiritual condition? How did He make the Word of God come alive? Take a moment to describe your experience. What impacted you most?

2. Who do you know whose mind has been "blinded by the god of this world" and desperately needs to hear and see the light of the Gospel? Take time to begin praying for them by name, asking the Holy Spirit to give them spiritual eyes to see and ears to hear the truth of Christ.

TOPIC

The Holy Spirit Guides

SCRIPTURES

1. **John 16:13** — Howbeit when he, the Spirit of truth, is come, he will guide you....
2. **Romans 8:14** — For as many as are led by the Spirit of God, they are the sons of God.

GREEK WORDS

1. "guide" — ὁδηγός (*hodegos*): a guide who shows a traveler the safest course through an unknown country; a guide who knows the safest, fastest, and most pleasurable route to take; a tour guide; a guide for the blind
2. "led" — ἄγω (*ago*): to lead: depicted animals led by a rope tied around their necks, that followed wherever their owner led them; the owner would "tug" and "pull" and the animal followed; to be led by a gentle tug or pull; this word forms the root for the Greek word ἀγών (*agon*), which describes an intense conflict, such as a struggle in a wrestling match or a struggle of the human will

SYNOPSIS

As noted in an earlier lesson, Jesus' last words to His disciples before being arrested, scourged, and crucified are recorded in detail in John 14, 15, and 16. Although He could have talked about a number of things — like the formation of the Church or end-time prophecy — Jesus spent His remaining moments with His closest companions describing the ministry of the Holy Spirit.

Four times, Jesus referred to the Holy Spirit as the *Comforter*, which means He is our full-time trainer and coach. Three times Jesus called Him the *Spirit of Truth*, which means the Holy Spirit can be thoroughly trusted, and He'll never lead you in the wrong direction. In fact, the

Scripture says, "Howbeit when he, the Spirit of truth, is come, he will guide you into all truth…" (John 16:13).

Take a moment and reread these powerful words from Jesus. "Howbeit when he, the Spirit of truth, is come, he will guide you into all truth…" (John 16:13). Friend, the Holy Spirit *is* God, and He knows everything about everything. If you will become a faithful apprentice — obeying His direction and receiving His correction — He will always lead and guide you into God's perfect will for your life.

The emphasis of this lesson:

Another role the Holy Spirit is called to play in our lives is that of a Divine Tour Guide. Our job is to learn to sense His leading and obey. Struggling to get our way and turning a deaf ear to His promptings can be disastrous. But if we will put our hand in His and let Him lead, our life's journey will be an enjoyable experience.

A Summary of the Ten Aspects of the Holy Spirit's Work

What does the Holy Spirit desire to do in your life and the life of every believer? Jesus made it clear that there are ten specific ways the Holy Spirit wants to help us walk through this life victoriously. As an abiding resident in our hearts, **the Holy Spirit has been sent to**…

Number 1: *Comfort* us (John 14:16).

Number 2: Permanently *indwell* us (John 14:17).

Number 3: *Teach* us all things (John 14:26).

Number 4: *Remind* us of all things (John 14:26).

Number 5: *Testify to* us and *through* us about who Jesus is (John 15:26).

Number 6: *Convict* us of sin (John 16:9).

Number 7: *Convince* us of righteousness (John 16:10).

Number 8: *Guide* us into all truth (John 16:13).

Number 9: *Reveal things* to us (John 16:13).

Number 10: *Help us worship* Jesus (John 16:14).

Just as Jesus is the exact image of the Father in Heaven, the Holy Spirit is the exact image of Jesus. When you have the Holy Spirit, you have the One who is just like Jesus. He thinks like Jesus thinks, talks like Jesus talked, and heals like Jesus healed. And He also *guides* us just like Jesus would *guide*.

NUMBER 8: THE HOLY SPIRIT *GUIDES* US

Let the Spirit Be Your Tour Guide

Looking once more at John 16:13, Jesus declared, "Howbeit when he, the Spirit of truth, is come, he will guide you into all truth...." The word "guide" in Greek is the word *hodegos*, which is taken from the word *hodas*, the term for a *road*. When *hodas* becomes *hodegos*, it describes *one who knows all the roads*. It is the Greek word for *a tour guide* — *one who shows a traveler the safest course through an unknown country*. This is a guide who knows the safest, fastest, and most pleasurable route to take.

What is interesting about this word *hodegos* — translated here as "guide" — is it's the same word used to describe *a guide for the blind*. If someone was blind, he had to put all his trust in his guide to lead him safely and correctly to where he needed to go. By using this word, Jesus is saying, "Let the Holy Spirit be your eyes. Trust Him. He is the Spirit of Truth and is able to see what you cannot see. He will never lead you astray."

It is no accident that Jesus chose the word *hodegos* (guide) to describe the work of the Holy Spirit. He is the greatest tour guide you will ever have. He knows all the roads and the best routes to take and the ones you need to avoid. If you let Him lead, He will take you on the most exciting, most enjoyable journey ever.

Realize you don't know the future, but the Holy Spirit does. Jesus said, "...He will guide you into all truth: for he shall not speak of himself; but whatsoever he shall hear, that shall he speak: and he will shew you things to come" (John 16:13). The Holy Spirit sees and knows the explicit will of God for your life and knows in advance how the enemy will attack you to try to derail you from your destiny. If you will obediently follow Him like an apprentice, He'll enable you to fulfill your divine calling.

Learn To Sense and Respond to His Gentle Prompting and Don't Struggle To Get Your Own Way

The fact that the Holy Spirit is our *Guide* brings us back to Romans 8:14, where Paul writes, "For as many as are led by the Spirit of God, they are the sons of God." The word "led" here is the Greek word *ago*, which means *to lead*, and it depicted animals led by a rope tied around their necks, who followed wherever their owner led them. The owner would "tug" or "pull," and the animal followed. Hence, the word *ago* indicates *being led by a gentle tug or pull.* Very often the leading of the Holy Spirit is a gentle tug or pull, and we must learn to become sensitive and responsive to His gentle ways.

What's interesting is that the word *ago* — translated here as "led" — also forms the root for the Greek word *agon*, which describes *an intense conflict*, such as a struggle in a wrestling match or a struggle of the human will. This word shows that sometimes when the Holy Spirit desires to lead us, our human will does not want to do what He's leading us to do. In those moments, it's like being thrown into a wrestling match in which our soul struggles against what the Lord is asking us to do.

In our spirit, we know the Holy Spirit is prompting us to do something, but our mind, will, and emotions tell us, *This is not right. I don't like the way this makes me feel, and I don't want to do it.* In moments like these, we must learn to stay in our place behind the Holy Spirit. We're not to be out front directing the Spirit! Our position is behind Him — following His lead, direction, and guidance. A mature believer has the ability to sense where the Lord is leading and then to follow that leading — even if that leading at the moment means to stay put! We must make it our goal to be the Holy Spirit's "tagalongs." This is truly where our life of adventure begins.

Listening to and Obeying the Holy Spirit Is Vital

Rick shared this personal story from the pages of his life that perfectly illustrates just how important it is to listen to and obey the promptings of the Holy Spirit when you sense He is leading you:

> "Many years ago, Denise and I were ministering in Chicago, and on one afternoon, we laid down to get some rest before we went to the evening service. As I lay on the bed, I began to be deeply disturbed in my heart and sensed I wasn't supposed to leave the

room that night. But my mind said, *Why would the Holy Spirit want me to stay in the room when I could go to the meeting and receive wonderful ministry?*

"As we got up and got dressed, I said to Denise, 'I don't know why, but I feel the Holy Spirit tugging on my heart, urging me not to leave this room tonight. I don't know why He would tell me to do that?'

"This war began between my heart and my head continued to rage, but I finally convinced myself that the thoughts to stay in the room were sheer nonsense. *This must be my imagination,* I thought. So I overrode the uneasiness in my spirit and made the decision to go to the meeting.

"As Denise and I rode across town to the church, the whole way there I was grieved and weighed down on the inside. Several times I turned to Denise and said, 'I don't know why, but I feel like this car needs to turn around and take me back to the hotel room. For some reason, I'm supposed to be in that room tonight.' Then my mind would kick in and reason it away, saying, *Nah, that doesn't make any sense. Why would God want me to sit in a room by myself when I could be in a great meeting receiving wonderful ministry?*

"Finally, we made it to the church where we greeted our friends with handshakes and hugs, but just as we all turned to walk into the auditorium for the meeting, the intensity of the inward grief became even stronger. In that moment, I said, 'Denise, I don't know what's going on, but for some reason I feel I'm supposed to be in our hotel room tonight. I feel like the Holy Spirit is telling me to go back to the room and get there as fast as I can. I cannot go into the service.'

"I quickly reconnected with our driver and asked him to please take me back to my hotel. As we made our way back across town, I realized I was going to miss dinner, so I asked the driver to pull into a fast-food restaurant so I could get something to eat. I then took my time and walked over to a nearby convenience store and bought some toothpaste and then slowly made my way back to the car.

"When I got back to the hotel and walked into the lobby, the receptionist said, 'Why are you back from the meeting so early?' Rather than try to explain to her about feeling led that I was supposed to be in my room, I chose to visit with her for a little while and then make my way to the elevator and back up to our room.

"At that point, a great deal of time had passed. When I finally turned the key in the door and walked into the room, it looked as though a whirlwind had come through. Our suitcases were opened, and our clothes were thrown around everywhere. Immediately, I noticed Denise's jewelry box had been tossed to the floor, and it was empty. Nothing left but some cheap custom jewelry scattered around.

"Frantic, I turned and looked over at the desk where I had left my computer and my briefcase. Both were now gone. Of all our possessions, these were extremely important. My briefcase contained my passport and all of our legal documents, and on my computer were five unpublished books that I was writing — and I had no additional copies.

"As I stood there in a state of shock and gazed around the room, it took me a few seconds to realize we had been robbed. Someone had come in after we had left and ransacked the room. They had gone through all our luggage and stolen my briefcase, my computer, and all of Denise's beautiful jewelry — some of which was brand new. Everything of value was taken, and we felt so violated.

"Instantly, I heard the still voice of the Holy Spirit say, *Now you know why I was leading you to stay in the room*. Wow! I learned a valuable lesson from that experience: Always listen to and obey the guiding voice of the Holy Spirit, and catastrophes like this can be avoided."

The Holy Spirit Knows Everything!

Remember, the Holy Spirit is your *Tour Guide* — your *hodegos*. He knows all the roads and is keenly aware of what's going to happen before it happens. He knows what's going to take place in the economy, on your job, in the weather, and around the world. He knows where you should invest your money and how you should educate your children. He knows the relationships you should cultivate and the relationships you should cut off. He knows when and where you should go — and when you should stay put. He knows what actions you need to take and what actions you should avoid. There's nothing that the Holy Spirit does not know.

If you will listen to the Spirit and follow His leading, you can effectively put a stop to what the enemy has planned for you. The Spirit will tug on your heart and direct you to make the healthiest choices you can make in every area of your life. He is the Spirit of Truth that you can fully trust. He will guide you in such a way that your life's journey will be a pleasurable experience.

Friend, it's time to stop trying to figure everything out by yourself and begin looking and listening for the divine guidance of the Holy Spirit. Yes, use your head and the common sense God gave you, but don't let your soul take control. Your mind, will, and emotions are flawed by sin and are no match for the perfect leadership of the Holy Spirit. If He says go, *go*. If He says stay, *stay*. Your job is to say, "Yes Sir!" and obey His promptings. Put your hand in His and trust Him to lead you.

In our next lesson, we'll examine how the Holy Spirit reveals things to us and how He worships Jesus through our lives.

STUDY QUESTIONS

Study to shew thyself approved unto God, a workman that needeth not to be ashamed, rightly dividing the word of truth.
— 2 Timothy 2:15

1. Trying to figure out everything in your life is both overwhelming and exhausting. The good news is — you don't have to! God has a proven remedy for this fruitless tendency and it is found in **Proverbs 3:5-8**. Look up these timeless words of wisdom in a few different Bible versions, and write out the version that comes alive in your heart.

2. Keep in mind that while your vision and knowledge is limited, the Holy Spirit sees and knows everything. He is your Guide and stands ready, willing, and able to direct you. Take time to chew on these promises from God's Word. What is the Holy Spirit showing you about making plans?
    *   **Proverbs 16:1 (*TLB*)** – "We can make our plans, but the final outcome is in God's hands."

- **Proverbs 16:9 (*AMPC*)** – "A man's mind plans his way, but the Lord directs his steps and makes them sure."

- **Proverbs 19:21 (*NIV*)** – "Many are the plans in a man's heart, but it is the Lord's purpose that prevails."

- **Proverbs 20:24 (*AMPC*)** – "Man's steps are ordered by the Lord. How then can a man understand his way?"

- **Psalm 127:1 (*NKJV*)** – "Unless the Lord builds the house, they labor in vain who build it...."

(Also consider James 4:13-16 and Proverbs 16:3.)

PRACTICAL APPLICATION

**But be ye doers of the word, and not hearers only,
deceiving your own selves.
—James 1:22**

1. Oftentimes, the leading of the Holy Spirit is *a gentle tug or pull*. Can you remember a time when you sensed the Spirit gently directing you to do or not do something? What was it? Did you follow His leading? What was the outcome of your actions and what did you learn from the situation?

2. There are also times when the Holy Spirit's leading is like a wrestling match in which our human will struggles to obey what He is asking us to do. Can you recall a situation like this? If so, what was the Holy Spirit prompting you to do? Did you obey His instruction? If you didn't, *why*? If you could go back and relive those moments, what would you do differently?

3. Be honest: Has the Holy Spirit been trying to guide you in a specific area, and you haven't listened to Him? What has He been asking you to do — or *not* do? How has this lesson put a reverential fear of God in you to repent for your inaction and begin obeying the Spirit's leading?

TOPIC

The Holy Spirit Reveals and Helps Us Worship

SCRIPTURES

1. **John 16:13** — Howbeit when he, the Spirit of truth, is come, he will guide you into all truth: for he shall not speak of himself; but whatsoever he shall hear, that shall he speak and he will shew you things to come.

2. **1 Corinthians 2:12** — Now we have received, not the spirit of the world, but the spirit which is of God; that we might know the things that are freely given to us of God.

3. **John 16:14** — He shall glorify me....

4. **John 4:23,24** — But the hour cometh, and now is, when the true worshipers shall worship the Father in spirit and in truth: for the Father seeketh such to worship him. God is a Spirit: and they that worship him must worship him in spirit and in truth.

5. **1 Corinthians 14:15 (*AMP*)** — Then what am I to do? I will pray with the spirit [by the Holy Spirit that is within me] and I will pray with the mind [using words I understand]; I will sing with the spirit [by the Holy Spirit that is within me] and I will sing with the mind [using words I understand].

6. **1 Thessalonians 5:23** — And the very God of peace sanctify you wholly; and I pray God your whole spirit and soul and body be preserved blameless unto the coming of our Lord Jesus Christ.

7. **1 Corinthians 6:19** — What? know ye not that your body is the temple of the Holy Ghost which is in you, which ye have of God, and ye are not your own?

GREEK WORDS

1. "shew" — ἀναγγέλλω (*anangello*): tell all the way up; from beginning to the conclusion; to fully tell or to fully show; even to rehearse

2. "know" — οἶδα (*oida*) to see, perceive, understand, or comprehend

3. "glorify" — δοξάζω (*doxadzo*): from δοκέω (*dokeo*), to think or to estimate; honor; value; to show weight and worth

4. "worship" — προσκυνέω (*proskuneo*): one who fell on the ground prostrate before a superior to worship or to collapse onto one's face or on one's knees in order to worship; worshipers who extended their arms toward a god in absolute love, affection, and devotion and even lovingly blew kisses toward that god; one who uses all available methods necessary to adore and worship a god

SYNOPSIS

Without question, the days in which we are living are unlike anything we have ever seen in human history. If there was ever a time we needed the supernatural insight of the Holy Spirit, it's now. Jesus said that one of the Spirit's jobs is to "…show you things to come" (John 16:13). In the Living Bible, this verse says, "…He will tell you about the future."

If you will surrender your life to the Holy Spirit and listen for His voice, He will reveal the details you need to know — when you need to know them. In doing so, He will keep you protected and provided for in these last days. And through the Spirit's power, He will teach you how to bring praise to Jesus, transforming your everyday life into ongoing worship that brings the Lord great glory.

The emphasis of this lesson:

The Holy Spirit has an accurate view of all things — past, present, and future. He will help us by revealing what we need to see and understand about God, ourselves, and life itself. The Holy Spirit is also designated by God to teach us how to worship Jesus and bring Him great honor and glory through our lives — spirit, soul, and body.

A Recap of the Ten Aspects of the Holy Spirit's Work

Isn't it interesting that every time Jesus spoke about the Holy Spirit, never once did He refer to the Spirit as an "it" or a feeling or a thing. Instead, Jesus always described the Holy Spirit with words like *He*, *Him*, and *Himself.* This confirms that the Holy Spirit is a Person — specifically, He is the third Person of the Trinity who is fully God and possesses all the same qualities as Jesus and the Father. It is this same Person who lives inside of you and desires to be intimately involved in your life.

In John's gospel, Jesus described ten specific things that the Holy Spirit is called to do in the life of every believer:

Number 1: The Holy Spirit *comforts* us (John 14:16).

Number 2: The Holy Spirit permanently *indwells* us (John 14:17).

Number 3: The Holy Spirit *teaches* us all things (John 14:26).

Number 4: The Holy Spirit *reminds* us of all things (John 14:26).

Number 5: The Holy Spirit *testifies to* us and *through* us about Jesus (John 15:26).

Number 6: The Holy Spirit *convicts* us of sin (John 16:9).

Number 7: The Holy Spirit *convinces* us we are righteous through Christ (John 16:10).

Number 8: The Holy Spirit *guides* us into all truth (John 16:13).

Number 9: The Holy Spirit *reveals things* to us (John 16:13).

Number 10: The Holy Spirit *helps us worship* (John 16:14).

As you begin to develop your relationship with the Holy Spirit and cooperate with His divine leadership, He will actively take on all these functions in your life — including His role as the great Revealer.

NUMBER 9: THE HOLY SPIRIT *REVEALS THINGS* TO US

His Ability To Reveal Things Is Limitless

In our last lesson, we saw how the Holy Spirit operates as our Divine Tour Guide who knows all the roads and wants to take us on the safest, fastest, most pleasurable route possible. We find this in John 16:13 where Jesus said, "Howbeit when he, the Spirit of truth, is come, he will guide you into all truth: for he shall not speak of himself; but whatsoever he shall hear, that shall he speak: and he will shew you things to come."

Notice the word "shew" in this verse. It is the Greek word *anangello*, and it means *to tell all the way up; from beginning to the conclusion*. It could also be translated *to fully tell* or *to fully show* or even *to rehearse*. Essentially, what Jesus is saying is that the Holy Spirit is a revealer that will show us the things that are yet to come, right up until the end of the age.

As the Spirit of Truth, the Holy Spirit has been given to…

- Reveal scriptural truth to us.
- Reveal everything we need to know for life.
- Reveal everything we need to know to have victory in our lives.

The truth is, without the Holy Spirit's involvement in our lives, we are walking in the dark the majority of the time, groping about aimlessly trying to turn on the light. It's a huge mistake to limit the work of the Holy Spirit to only scriptural and spiritual matters. His ability to reveal things to you is limitless!

Writing about the gift of the Holy Spirit, the apostle Paul said, "Now we have received, not the spirit of the world, but the spirit which is of God; that we might know the things that are freely given to us of God" (1 Corinthians 2:12). The word "know" in this verse is the Greek word *oida*, which means *to see, perceive, understand,* or *comprehend.* God wants you to see and understand many things regarding personal issues, scriptural truths, as well as practical and spiritual things. And it's the Holy Spirit's job to reveal them. He wants to remove the blinders and shine the light on every dark place, revealing what you need to know.

The Holy Spirit Shows Us Things That Are Keeping Us From Experiencing God's Best

For example, on a practical level, the Holy Spirit may reveal an upcoming financial attack of the enemy. If you're looking and listening for the Spirit's leading, you will feel His nudging in your spirit to do certain things to be prepared for or know how to circumvent the enemy's plan.

Likewise, the Holy Spirit may also reveal to you why you haven't been healed of an illness you've been fighting against — or why a habit still holds you hostage. He may show you a deadly root in your heart that must first be addressed and removed. It may be a secret sin you're protecting or unforgiveness you're holding toward someone that's keeping you from receiving your healing. The Spirit is not showing you these things to condemn you. He's revealing them to you so you can repent and make the needed adjustments in your life to be healed and delivered.

Keep in mind that Jesus called the Holy Spirit the "Comforter," which in Greek is the word *parakletos.* It is a compound of the word *para*, meaning *alongside*, and a form of the word *kaleo*, which means *to call out to*. Thus, the Holy Spirit will come right alongside you and tell you everything you need to know to turn your problem into a victory! Again, He sees things we cannot see and is able to reveal things that are hindering us from experiencing the abundant life of victory Jesus promised (*see* John 10:10; Romans 8:37).

Oftentimes we are unable to see all the facts or have a comprehensive view of ourselves, of others, and of what is really going on around us. But the Holy Spirit *does* have a very precise, accurate view of everything. He wants to show you what you need to see, but He needs your listening ear and humble heart to hear and receive what He has to say. All you have to do is pray and say, "Holy Spirit, You are my Revealer, and I can't make it without You. Please show me everything I need to know in order to experience freedom and victory in this situation. In Jesus' name. Amen."

NUMBER 10: THE HOLY SPIRIT *HELPS US WORSHIP*

Our Actions Are To Bring Jesus Glory

What else does the Holy Spirit do in our lives as believers? Jesus said in John 16:14, "He shall glorify me...." The word "glorify" in Greek is *doxadzo*, which is from the word *dokeo*, meaning *to think* or *to estimate*. It is a term signifying *honor* or *value*. It means *to show weight and worth to someone or something*. In this verse, Jesus tells us that one of the chief responsibilities of the Holy Spirit is to bring Jesus great honor and value and show how worthy He is. And the vessel He chooses to glorify Jesus through is *you*!

How does the Spirit fulfill His responsibility to glorify Jesus Christ through you? Every time He heals the sick through you, Jesus gets glory! When He casts out demons through you, when He leads lost people to Jesus through you, and when He encourages the hopeless through you, Jesus is glorified in a magnificent way. Through acts like these, Christ is worshiped.

What It Means To 'Worship' God

As Jesus spoke to the Samaritan woman at the well just outside the city of Sychar, He made this powerful proclamation: "The hour cometh, and now is, when the true worshippers shall worship the Father in spirit and in truth: for the Father seeketh such to worship him. God is a Spirit: and they that worship him must worship him in spirit and in truth" (John 4:23,24).

In these two verses, Jesus used the word "worship" five times. In Greek, the word "worship" is *proskuneo*, which is a compound of the words *pros* and *kuneo*. The word *pros* means *toward* and describes *very close* or *intimate contact*. The word *kuneo* means *to kiss* or *to blow kisses*. When these two words are compounded into one, they form the word *proskuneo*, which means *to fall on the ground toward someone and to kiss*. During the time that the New Testament was being written, the Greek word *proskuneo* (worship) was especially used to depict one who fell on the ground prostrate before a superior to worship or to collapse onto one's face or on one's knees in order to worship.

When used to depict a person's worshipful position before the Lord, the word *proskuneo* pictures one who has prostrated himself, either outwardly or inwardly, bowing on his knees or in his heart before God to worship in intimate adoration. This word pictures *one who uses all available methods necessary to adore and worship God*. This includes singing, playing musical instruments, dancing, or using movements, gestures, or words to convey one's worship. These worshipers have fallen into a place of close intimacy with God, and all of their acts of affection toward God are straight from the heart.

True Worship Involves One's Spirit, Soul, and Body

In John 4:23 and 24, the use of this word *proskuneo* — translated as "worship" — tells us that God seeks those who worship Him with the mind, the body, and the spirit. Authentic worship includes an intellectual dimension, a physical dimension, and a spiritual dimension. No one made this clearer than the apostle Paul in his first letter to the Corinthians. He wrote:

> **Then what am I to do? I will pray with the spirit [by the Holy Spirit that is within me] and I will pray with the mind [using words I understand]; I will sing with the spirit [by the Holy Spirit that is within me] and I will sing with the mind [using words I understand].**
> **— 1 Corinthians 14:15 (*AMP*)**

Paul stated that real worship is both *spiritual* and *intellectual*. It involves the spirit *and* the mind. The fact is, each of us is a three-part being, and this is clearly seen in First Thessalonians 5:23, which says, "And the very God of peace sanctify you wholly; and I pray God your whole spirit and soul and body be preserved blameless unto the coming of our Lord Jesus Christ."

God has made us spirit, soul, and body. As three-part beings, every part of us is to be involved in worship. Through our body, we worship God in the physical dimension. With our soul, we worship God on an intellectual dimension. And with our spirit, we worship Him in a spiritual dimension.

You Are God's Temple of Worship

God has placed His own Spirit inside us as believers. So we do not have to find a physical building to enter into worship. We *are* the *temple* of God! Paul declares this in First Corinthians 6:19 and in other places throughout his writings.

The Holy Spirit has made us inwardly so fabulous that He was pleased to move in, settle down, and permanently take up residency in our hearts — and we became His temple. At the moment of your new birth, you became a walking sanctuary, and your spirit became a temple containing the very presence of God Himself. If your eyes were opened to see your spiritual interior, you would be shocked to view how marvelously adorned your heart is spiritually!

The Christian does not go to a temple to worship. The Christian takes the temple with him or her. As temples of the Holy Spirit, we are in position to launch into worship at any time, at any place, and at any moment of the day — whenever we choose to humbly bow our hearts to God in worship-ful adoration.

How glorious to realize we don't have to go to a physical location to worship because we are now the sanctuary of God on this earth! And the Holy Spirit — the greatest worship leader of all — is living inside us at all times! He loves to worship Jesus, and if we will humbly surrender our-selves — spirit, soul, and body — He will worship the Lord through us. In every situation, He will prompt us on how to move our hands and feet and tell us what words to speak and songs to sing. The important thing is to be a yielded vessel in His hands that follows His leading.

Worship Is More Than a Song

Please realize, that worship is not merely about music, talent, or performance. The act of worship occurs when we reach a point of abandonment in His presence — when we focus solely on Jesus and are lost in adoration of Him. As we do this, our worship ascends to Him like loving, intimate kisses upon His face. When God receives such worship, the Scripture shows that it touches Him deeply. He enters into the midst of it and becomes a part of what is happening. That is the moment when the atmosphere is charged with a power that transforms the worshipers.

In our next lesson, we will take a close look at Paul's words in Ephesians 4 and learn what it means to grieve the Holy Spirit.

STUDY QUESTIONS

Study to shew thyself approved unto God, a workman that needeth
not to be ashamed, rightly dividing the word of truth.
— 2 Timothy 2:15

1. There is a very important quality about God that is repeated all throughout Scripture — including Jeremiah 17:10; First Chronicles 28:9; Proverbs 21:2; Romans 8:27; and Revelation 2:23. What is this divine ability that only God has? What did David pray in Psalm 139:23 and 24 in connection with this ability that we should also pray on a regular basis?

2. It is a huge mistake to limit the work of the Holy Spirit to only scriptural and spiritual matters. His ability to reveal things to you is limitless! Carefully reflect on Jeremiah 33:3; Matthew 7:7-11; First Corinthians 2:9,10,12; and Ephesians 3:20 and share how these passages expand your understanding of what God is capable of revealing to you.

3. Take a few moments to reread the section on the meaning of the word "worship" — the Greek word *proskueno*. In your own words, describe what it means to *worship* God. In what practical ways are you bringing Jesus glory through your life? How are you worshiping Him in your spirit, soul, and body?

PRACTICAL APPLICATION

> But be ye doers of the word, and not hearers only,
> deceiving your own selves.
> —James 1:22

1. The Holy Spirit is the *revealer* of all things. What do you need answers for right now? Is it overcoming anger or fear? Are you struggling to reconnect with your spouse and see restoration in your marriage? Are you trying to get out from under a black cloud of depression and hopelessness?

    • Take a few moments and tell the Holy Spirit what you need help with.

    • Now ask Him to show you what you need to know about *God*, *yourself*, and *your situation* in order to see victory.

    • What specific action steps do you feel the Holy Spirit is asking you to take at this time?

2. If you've been dealing with an ongoing illness you can't seem to shake or a habit that continues to hold you hostage, stop and pray: *Holy Spirit, is there something in my heart keeping me from receiving a breakthrough in my life? If so, please reveal it to me and show me what I need to do to deal with it. In Jesus' name. Amen.*

LESSON 9

TOPIC

The Holy Spirit Can Be Grieved

SCRIPTURES

1. **James 4:4** — Ye adulterers and adulteresses, know ye not that friendship of the world is enmity with God? Whosoever therefore will be a friend of the world is the enemy of God.

2. **Ephesians 4:26-31** — Be ye angry, and sin not: let not the sun go down upon your wrath: neither give place to the devil. Let him that stole steal no more: but rather let him labour, working with his hands the thing which is good, that he may have to give to him that needeth.

Let no corrupt communication proceed out of your mouth, but that which is good to the use of edifying, that it may minister grace unto the hearers. And grieve not the holy Spirit of God, whereby ye are sealed unto the day of redemption. Let all bitterness, and wrath, and anger, and clamour, and evil speaking, be put away from you, with all malice.

3. **James 4:6** — But he giveth more grace. Wherefore he saith, God resisteth the proud, but giveth grace unto the humble.

GREEK WORDS

1. "friendship" — **φιλία** (*philia*): friendship, affection, fondness, love; an intense fondness that is developed between people who enjoy each other's company; two or more people who know one another, who are fond of one another, and who are growing more deeply involved in each other's lives

2. "world" — **κόσμος** (*kosmos*): the world; depicts anything fashioned or ordered; denotes systems and institutions in society, such as fashion, finances, education, entertainment; world systems

3. "will be" — **βούλομαι** (*boulomai*): counsel or resolve

4. "grieve" — **λύπη** (*lupete*): pain or grief; depicts shock, devastation, hurt, wounds, and grief; depicts something that is painful, sorrowful, filled with anguish, torment, or agony; depicts the emotions felt when spousal unfaithfulness occurs

5. "is" — **καθίστημι** (*kathistemi*): to constitute or to render

6. "resisteth" — **ἀντιτάσσομαι** (*antitassomai*): to arrange oneself against; to methodically oppose; a strategic plan of opposition intended to bring a situation under control

SYNOPSIS

So far in our study we have established that the Holy Spirit is God's gift to us, and He enters into our life the moment we repent of our sin and surrender ourselves to Jesus. The Holy Spirit is exactly like Jesus in every way, and He functions as our coach, trainer, guide, and teacher — revealing things to us we need to know about God, about ourselves, about others, and about our situations. He gives us His all every day, and He wants us to give our all to Him.

Actually, the Bible says, "…The Holy Spirit, whom God has placed within us, watches over us with tender jealousy" (James 4:5 *TLB*). The Holy Spirit is the lover of our soul, and He wants our attention and affection exclusively. Although He will never leave us, our actions can sometimes grieve Him and cause Him to draw back and stop manifesting His power and presence in our lives.

The emphasis of this lesson:

The things that most grieve the Holy Spirit are ungodly treatment of others and giving our attention and affection to the things of this world rather than to Him. To avoid grieving the Spirit, we need to maintain our passion for Him and learn how to honor His presence in every area of our daily lives.

James Called His Readers 'Adulterers and Adulteresses'

The book of James is a short read filled with practical principles for everyday living. It was written by James, the half-brother of Jesus, to a group of Jewish Christians living in the First Century. Even before they came to faith in Christ, James' readers were good, God-fearing people. Yet when we come to the fourth chapter, we find that they had somehow drifted from their original devotion to Jesus. This fact becomes extremely evident in James 4:4, which says:

> **Ye adulterers and adulteresses, know ye not that friendship of the world is enmity with God? whosoever therefore will be a friend of the world is the enemy of God.**

Can you imagine the shock that this group of believers must have felt when James leveled the charge of adultery against them? This is a strong accusation! Even before they came to Christ, these Jews would never think of committing adultery. Adulterers and adulteresses were stoned to death under Jewish law. James couldn't have said anything more shocking, hurtful, or outrageous to these Jewish believers!

So, since they were moral people who would never actually commit adultery, why did James call them adulterers and adulteresses? It's because these believers had crossed a line somewhere along the way and had been drawn into an improper relationship with the world. In a spiritual sense, they were beginning to give their hearts to other things, and their devotion to the Lord was diminishing. To get their attention and drive this very serious point into their hearts, James called them *adulterers* and *adulteresses*.

The word "adultery" has all kinds of connotations, such as *unfaithfulness*, *impurity*, and *the violation of a commitment to marriage*. We normally associate adultery with a spouse who has engaged in a sexual relationship outside of his or her marriage. When this betrayal of the marriage covenant is discovered, the violated spouse feels such deep hurt that nothing else in the world can be compared to it. Even the death of a spouse can be less difficult to process than the betrayal of a husband or wife who has committed adultery.

The Pain of Unfaithfulness in Marriage Is Excruciating

Rick shared about when he and Denise were first married, they were ministers for the single adults in a large denominational church. They had developed a program to help those who were newly divorced, and in one year's time, they ministered to approximately 1,100 people who had been through a divorce.

Although it was one of the most rewarding experiences of their early ministry, it was also very troubling. Seeing people who had been so rejected and wounded being healed by the power of Jesus Christ was certainly gratifying. But it was also difficult for them to repeatedly hear the outpouring of agonizing emotions that those precious people went through as a result of being betrayed by someone they trusted.

Out of the hundreds of cases they heard, about two-thirds of them sounded identical. Time and again, emotionally broken people said things like, "I just don't know how he/she could do that to me! After all these years of being faithful, raising our children together, and working to help him/her through school — *how could he/she do this to me?* I gave the best I knew how. How could he/she dump me and go after someone else? I feel like my heart has been ripped out and stomped on! I feel like I've been kicked in the gut and had the wind knocked out of me."

Indeed, infidelity by a spouse is possibly the worst betrayal of all in the human experience. Nothing seems to hurt worse, cut deeper, or last longer than this kind of betrayal. Feelings of deep grieving, rejection, and the hurt of being lied to, misled and deceived can threaten to emotionally consume a person in that situation. These are just some of the terribly strong and painful emotions a spouse feels when the sanctity and security of the marriage relationship has been recklessly thrown away by the adulterer or adulteress.

What Does It Mean To Be a 'Friend of the World'?

When James spoke to his Jewish Christian readers, in the original Greek text he addressed them simply as "adulteresses." The word "adulterers" does not appear. This tells us he was writing specifically to the members of the Church, which is the Bride of Christ. In some way that James doesn't describe, these believers had gone outside their relationship with Christ to find fulfillment and companionship with someone or something else. They were giving their minds, hearts, and lives to worldly things. Their devotion and focus had shifted away from Jesus, and it was grieving the Holy Spirit. They had been unfaithful to their "Spouse," Jesus Christ; hence, James called them "adulteresses."

Sin affects not only us individually, but also the indwelling Holy Spirit. He actually feels hurt and grief, as of a violated spouse. When this truth becomes revelation to our hearts, it will change our permissive attitude toward sin and cause us to live more consecrated lives for Jesus Christ.

Again, James said, "Ye adulterers and adulteresses, know ye not that friendship of the world is enmity with God? Whosoever therefore will be a friend of the world is the enemy of God" (James 4:4). Notice the word "friendship" in this verse. It is the Greek word *philia*, which describes *friendship, affection, fondness,* or *love.* It is an intense fondness that is developed between people who enjoy each other's company. It refers to two or more people who know one another, who are fond of one another, and who are growing more deeply involved in each other's lives.

This word *philia* — translated here as "friendship" — conveys the idea of a friend with whom you desire to have a deeper relationship. In a certain sense, this attraction is so great that it leads to being preoccupied with that someone or something. It involves giving attention, time, devotion, and focus to that person. That is precisely the condition James was talking about when he addressed these believers. They had pulled away from the Lord and began giving their attention, time, and devotion to worldly things.

Please understand, James wasn't judging these believers for having expensive tastes, working at good jobs, or desiring nice houses. The phrase "friendship of the world" was not about owning things — it was about being *consumed* or *preoccupied* with the things of this world. Those to whom James wrote his epistle were getting tangled up in the thinking, the behavior, and material possessions of the world.

The 'World' Refers to the Systems and Institutions of Society

This brings us to the word "world" in James 4:4, which is a form of the Greek word *kosmos*, meaning *the world*. Specifically, it depicts anything *fashioned* or *ordered*. It denotes systems and institutions in society, such as fashion, finances, education, and entertainment. Essentially, it is world systems.

It appears that these believers who were once on fire for Jesus were being seduced and swallowed up by the things of the world. This process of seduction had progressed to the point of their being attracted to, consumed with, and preoccupied with the world. This attraction had become so great that they entered into friendship with the world. They had gone outside of their relationship with Christ to give their hearts and minds to something else. They had committed spiritual adultery.

Flirting with the world eventually leads to an ungodly connection with the things of the world. It is spiritual adultery to be *so involved* with the current status quo of society that you begin to think as they do, act as they do, and seek the same things they do. Yes, we live in the world and are going to be here until the rapture takes place or we die and go to Heaven. Therefore, we will need to have a job, secure a home and transportation, purchase food and clothing, and cultivate relationships. All these things are in the world. Having things of the world in your hand is one thing. But when the things of the world leave your hand and get into your heart and you become preoccupied with them, you have crossed a serious line.

Beware of 'Self-Counseling' Yourself Into Catastrophe

Note that James said, "…Whosoever therefore will be a friend of the world is the enemy of God" (James 4:4). The words "will be" are a form of the Greek word *boulomai*, which describes *counsel* or *resolve*. It depicts a counseling session or seeking the counsel of someone else. In this particular verse, the word *boulomai* doesn't describe some other counselor listening to you and advising you. In this case the counselor is *you* — and you are counseling yourself. It presents a picture of a Christian being seduced by the world.

Rather than saying a firm *no* to ungodliness, this believer willingly chooses to draw nearer to the world for a closer look. This Christian feels his flesh being lured by the world. When he senses the warning of the Holy Spirit to withdraw from the situation and walk in holiness, he turns a deaf ear to the Spirit in order to listen to his flesh. Before long, he is talking himself into doing what he knows is wrong.

He may think to himself, *Well, I know I shouldn't, but just a little won't hurt. I know I'm not as on fire for God as I used to be, and I know it will probably grieve the Holy Spirit. But God will forgive me. I can't believe I'm doing this, and I know I shouldn't. But just this one time....* This Christian literally talks — or "counsels" — himself into doing what he knows is wrong. It's a process that is seductive and deceptive.

In essence, James was saying, "If you've become the friend of the world, here's the reason: You've made so many little exceptions for yourself that now what used to bother you doesn't bother you at all. In fact, over a period of time, you've become a worldly Christian with worldly thinking and worldly behavior!"

Being a friend to the world doesn't happen overnight. It takes time. It's what we call *backsliding*. Very slowly — seductively and methodically — our thinking, our behavior, and our outlook grows to look more and more similar to that of the world than to that of Jesus. A little self-talk here, a little self-talk there, each time counseling ourselves into making one exception after another and moving further and further away from what we know in our heart is right. If we continue down this road, we will eventually abandon reading the Bible, praying, going to church, and being a witness to others.

Please realize, worldliness tries to wrap its arms around all of us. Not one of us is exempt from its seductive pull. It tries to lure the soul to lay aside godly convictions and follow the dictates of the flesh, indulging in pleasures that last only for a moment. We could all admit a tendency toward worldliness in some area of our lives. But if we don't deal with these areas as the Holy Spirit leads us, over time we will become more conformed to the world than to Jesus Christ.

The words "will be" — taken from the Greek word *boulomai*, which here describes *self-counsel* — clearly indicate that our spiritual condition is *our* responsibility. Just as a husband and wife need to work on their marital relationship, we need to work on our spiritual relationship with Jesus. We need to fan the flames of our love for Him and keep the fire burning brightly. This includes regularly investing time, attention, and energy into expressing our affection and gratefulness for all that He is. If we want to avoid the pain of grieving the Holy Spirit, we need to guard ourselves from being sucked into the seductive ways of the world.

To 'Grieve' the Holy Spirit Is To Cause Him Pain, Sorrow, and Agony

James is not the only person who wrote about grieving the Holy Spirit. Paul wrote about it too. In Ephesians 4:30, he said, "And grieve not the holy Spirit of God, whereby ye are sealed unto the day of redemption." The word "grieve" in this verse is *lupete*, a form of the Greek word *lupe*, which describes *pain* or *grief*. It depicts *shock, devastation, hurt, wounds,* and *grief*, something that is painful, sorrowful, filed with anguish, torment, or agony.

This word *lupete* — translated here as "grieve" — was used to denote the emotions of a betrayed spouse when spousal unfaithfulness occurs. Feeling betrayed, deceived, lied to, misled, hurt, wounded, and abused — all of these vividly portray the emotions of a spouse who has discovered that his or her mate has been unfaithful. This is the very word the apostle Paul used in Ephesians 4:30 to describe how we affect the indwelling Holy Spirit when we tend toward worldliness.

The use of this word is the equivalent of the Holy Spirit saying, "After all I've done for you, this is how you're going to treat Me? I've washed away your sins in the blood of Jesus, come into your heart to permanently live, cleaned you up and sanctified you, renewed your mind, gave you power and life, produced My fruit in you, worked My gifts in you and through you, and now you're going to violate your commitment to Me by giving yourself to other things and to other people, putting Me in second place when I used to have first place in your life?"

This is a very strong word of correction that Paul spoke to the church of Ephesus. But just what were these Ephesian believers doing that grieved the Holy Spirit so deeply? The Bible says...

1. They were *lying* (Ephesians 4:25).
2. They had *anger issues* and were letting the sun go down on their wrath (Ephesians 4:26).
3. They were *giving place to the devil* (Ephesians 4:27).
4. They were *stealing* (Ephesians 4:28).
5. They were *allowing corrupt communication to come out of their mouth* (Ephesians 4:29).
6. They were *filled with bitterness, wrath, anger, clamor, evil speaking, and malice* (Ephesians 4:31).

With all these attitudes and actions, it's no wonder the Holy Spirit was *grieved!*

The fact that Paul used the word "grieve" (*lupete*) tells us the Holy Spirit felt wounded by the wrong behavior and attitudes of certain believers. He felt like a spouse who was being dragged through the mud by an unfaithful mate. After all He had done within these believers to help them grow and become more like Jesus, how could they now push the Holy Spirit aside and give in to their flesh in such a manner?

Cultivate a 'Holy' Environment for the Holy Spirit

We need to think before we talk and act. We need to remember that Someone lives inside us whose name is the *Holy Spirit*. He is called the Holy Spirit because He is *holy*. In fact, the Bible says He is the *Spirit of Holiness* (*see* Romans 1:4). That is who He is, and that is what He comes to produce in our lives. When we behave in the ways Paul wrote about in Ephesians 4:25-31, we grieve the Holy Spirit. Instead of grieving the Spirit, we need to make every effort to cultivate a holy environment for Him to live and thrive in.

Friend, we need the Holy Spirit's presence in our lives. We need His divine partnership and the manifestation of His power. Apart from Him, we can do nothing (*see* John 15:5). But with Him and through His abiding strength, we can do all things!

In our final lesson, we will continue our study in the book of James and examine the Holy Spirit's deep desire to be welcomed in our lives.

STUDY QUESTIONS

**Study to shew thyself approved unto God, a workman that needeth
not to be ashamed, rightly dividing the word of truth.
— 2 Timothy 2:15**

1. Take a few moments to reflect on the meaning of the word "friend-
    ship"— the Greek word *philia*. In your own words, describe what
    "friendship with the world" might look like in your own life. Have you
    ever experienced this kind of worldly attraction and entanglement?
    Are you ensnared by it right now?

2. According to the Greek meanings in James 4:4, the reason many
    believers develop a "friendship with the world" is because they are
    self-counseling themselves into doing what they know is wrong. Be
    honest: Is this happening in your life? If so, where are you backslid-
    ing? What do you know in your heart you need to do to silence the
    wrong voices and listen to God's voice? How can you guard yourself
    from being sucked into the seductive ways of the world? (Consider
    Second Corinthians 6:14-18; Isaiah 52:11; Ephesians 5:11; Second
    Thessalonians 3:6.)

PRACTICAL APPLICATION

**But be ye doers of the word, and not hearers only,
deceiving your own selves.
— James 1:22**

1. James called his readers *adulterers* and *adulteresses* because they had
    crossed a line somewhere along the way and had been drawn into an
    improper relationship with the world. How about you? How strong
    is your hunger for Jesus? Are you passionately pursuing the Lord, or
    have you given your heart and mind to other things?

2. If your fire of desire for Jesus has grown cold, what has taken His
    place? Stop and take a look at your life, asking yourself and honestly
    answering these questions: *What has my attention? What activity fills
    my schedule and where am I spending a great deal of time and money?
    What am I thinking and talking about a great deal of the time? Am I
    tolerating things in my life today that I would never have tolerated five or
    ten years ago? If so, what are they?*

3. In Jesus' words of warning and correction to the church of Ephesus, He let them know He was deeply grieved because they had left their first love (*see* Revelation 2:4). What did Jesus tell these believers to do in Revelation 2:5 to rekindle the fire of love for Him they once had? In what practical ways can you apply Jesus' words to your own life? Pray and ask the Holy Spirit, *What do I need to do right now in order to deal with these issues and rededicate myself to passionately pursuing Jesus?*

TOPIC

The Desire of the Holy Spirit

SCRIPTURES

1. **James 4:4-6** — Ye adulterers and adulteresses, know ye not that friendship of the world is enmity with God? whosoever therefore will be a friend of the world is the enemy of God. Do ye think that the scripture saith in vain, The spirit that dwelleth in us lusteth to envy? But he giveth more grace. Wherefore he saith, God resisteth the proud, but giveth grace unto the humble.

GREEK WORDS

1. "will be" — βούλομαι (*boulomai*): counsel or resolve
2. "is" — καθίστημι (*kathistemi*): to constitute or to render
3. "dwelleth" — κατοικέω (*katoikeo*): depicts settling down into a new home and making oneself to feel comfortable there; a permanent resident
4. "in" — ἐν (*en*): in or inside
5. "lusteth" — ἐπιποθέω (*epipotheo*): an intense desire; a craving, a hunger, an ache, a yearning or hankering for something; a longing or pining for something; to strain after, to greatly desire; to have strong affection; a fervent passion; an obsession
6. "envy" — φθόνος (*phthonos*): jealousy; a hostile feeling toward someone else because of an advantage, benefit, or position that another has; a deeply felt grudge due to someone possessing what one wishes was

his own; to begrudge what another person possesses; to resent another person's possession or position and to try to find a way to seize it away from another person in order to make it his own

7. "resisteth" — ἀντιτάσσομαι (*antitassomai*): to arrange oneself against; to methodically oppose; a strategic plan of opposition intended to bring a situation under control

SYNOPSIS

When a person repents of his or her sin and invites Jesus Christ into his or her life, instantly that relationship with the Father is restored. If you have surrendered your life to Jesus and made Him the Lord of your life, you, too, are in right standing with God, and as a down payment on all the indescribably great things He has prepared for your life, God has given you the gift of His Spirit to permanently live inside of you. You are a temple of the Holy Spirit!

It's so important to realize that the Holy Spirit is not an "it" or a feeling or goosebumps. He is the third Person of the Trinity who is fully God and the greatest friend you will ever have. He is your Comforter, your Teacher, your Guide, and the reminder and revealer of all things. He testifies to you and through about Jesus. He convicts you of sin and convinces you that you are the righteousness of God in Christ. He is your Divine Coach and Trainer who yearns to be welcome in every area of your life.

The emphasis of this lesson:

The Holy Spirit permanently dwells inside you, and He yearns with great desire to have all of you for Himself. When you walk and talk like unbelievers and give your life to other things, the Holy Spirit feels like a jealous Lover who has been robbed. He will do everything in His power to regain your affection and drive His competition out of the picture.

A REVIEW OF LESSON 9

James Called His Listeners 'Adulteresses'

As we saw in our previous lesson, the book of James was written to a group of Christian Jews who were moral, God-fearing people even before they came to Christ. But somehow they had strayed away from their original devotion to Jesus. For this reason, James wrote to them and said:

Ye adulterers and adulteresses, know ye not that friendship of the world is enmity with God? whosoever therefore will be a friend of the world is the enemy of God.

—James 4:4

To call this group of believers *adulterers* and *adulteresses* was a strong and highly offensive accusation! These Jews would have never thought of committing adultery. Yet, the reason James addressed them so harshly was because these believers had violated their relationship with Jesus and the Holy Spirit. They had crossed a line somewhere in their journey and had been drawn into an improper relationship with the world. In a spiritual sense, they were beginning to give their hearts to other things, and their devotion to the Lord was diminishing.

What's interesting is that in the original Greek text, only the word "adulteresses" appears. This lets us know James was writing specifically to the members of the Church, which is the Bride of Christ. In some way, these believers had gone outside their relationship with Christ to find fulfillment and companionship with someone or something else. They were giving their minds, hearts, and lives to worldly things. Their devotion and focus had shifted away from Jesus, and it was grieving the Holy Spirit. They had been unfaithful to their "Spouse," Jesus Christ; hence, James called them *"adulteresses."*

Becoming a 'Friend' of the World Is Deadly

James said, "...Friendship of the world is enmity with God..." (James 4:4) The word "friendship" here is the Greek word *philia*, which describes *friendship, affection, fondness,* or *love.* It refers to two or more people who know one another, who become intensely fond of one another, and who are growing more deeply involved in each other's lives. In this case, James is describing the increasing fondness and love that was developing between these Jewish Christians and the world.

The word "world" is a form of the Greek word *kosmos*, and it depicts *systems and institutions in society,* such as fashion, finances, education, and entertainment. It could also be translated as worldliness. Apparently, the believers James had written to — who were once sold out to Jesus — had become attracted to, consumed with, and preoccupied with the world. This attraction had become so great their focus had moved off of Christ and onto the things of the world. And because they were giving their hearts and minds to something else, they had committed spiritual adultery.

James went on to say, "…Whosoever therefore will be a friend of the world is the enemy of God" (James 4:4). We saw that the words "will be" are a translation of the Greek word *boulomai*, which describes *counsel* or *resolve*. It is the word used to describe *a counseling session*, but in this verse, it doesn't describe a person receiving counsel from someone else. In this case, it depicts one who is counseling himself. It is the picture of a Christian being seduced by the world.

When this Christian feels his flesh being lured by the world, rather than saying a firm *no* to ungodliness, he chooses to draw nearer to the world for a closer look. When he senses the warning of the Holy Spirit to withdraw from the situation and walk in holiness, he turns a deaf ear to the Spirit in order to listen to the *counsel* of his flesh. Before long, he is talking himself into believing it is alright to violate his relationship with Jesus.

The Process Is Gradual, Seductive, and Deceiving

Being a friend to the world doesn't happen overnight. It takes time. No one wakes up one morning and says, "Today is the day I'm going to *backslide*." Very slowly — seductively and methodically — our thinking, our behavior, and our outlook grows to look more and more like the world than that of Jesus. A little self-talk here, a little self-talk there, we make one exception after another and move further and further away from what we know in our heart is right. We begin watching things we shouldn't watch, going places we shouldn't go, and saying things we shouldn't say.

Please realize worldliness tries to wrap its tentacles around all of us. Not one of us is exempt from its seductive pull. It tries to lure the soul to lay aside godly convictions and follow the dictates of the flesh, indulging in pleasures that last only for a moment. The truth is, we all have a tendency toward worldliness in some area of our lives. But if we don't deal with these areas as the Holy Spirit leads us, over time we will become more conformed to the world than to Jesus Christ.

The use of the word *boulomai* — translated here as "will be" and describing *self-counsel* — clearly indicates that our spiritual condition is *our* responsibility. Just as a husband and wife need to work on their marital relationship, we need to work on our spiritual relationship with Jesus. If we want to avoid the pain of grieving the Holy Spirit, we need to guard ourselves from being sucked into the seductive ways of the world.

There's one more word to consider as we seek to understand what James is saying, and it's the word "is." The Bible says, "…Whosoever therefore will be a friend of the world *is* the enemy of God" (James 4:4). The word "is" here means *to constitute* or *to render*. Thus, Christians who choose a worldly path *constitute* — or *establish* — themselves in direct opposition to God and become His enemies. And to be an enemy of God, means that God Himself will oppose you. No one in their right mind would want to be in such a deadly place of hostility.

Remember, the Holy Spirit Is a Permanent Indweller

When we come to the very next verse in James' letter, we see why this is so serious in God's eyes. It says, "Do ye think that the scripture saith in vain, The spirit that dwelleth in us lusteth to envy?" (James 4:5) There are four very important words in this verse we need to understand, and the first one is the word "dwelleth."

In Greek, the word "dwelleth" is the word *katoikeo*, which is a compound of the word *kata*, meaning *down*, and the word *oikeo*, meaning *to live* or *reside*. When these two words are joined together to form the word *katoikeo*, it depicts *one settling down into a new home and making oneself feel comfortable there*. It is the picture of *a permanent resident*.

This confirms what we learned earlier in our study: When the Holy Spirit comes to live inside us, He becomes a *permanent indweller*. We are not a hotel He comes to visit every now and then. We are His temple where He makes Himself at home. The Scripture says, "…The spirit dwelleth in us…" (James 4:5). Even the word "in" is significant. It is the Greek word *en*, which means *in* or *inside*. The Holy Spirit lives permanently inside us and has no intention of leaving.

The Spirit Craves You Intensely

Once the Holy Spirit has made Himself at home inside you, He begins to take on all the various functions we have studied in this series. This includes Him being your Comforter, your Teacher, and your Guide who desires to lead you into all truth. And the Holy Spirit takes His job very seriously, which is why the Bible says, "…The spirit that dwelleth in us lusteth to envy" (James 4:5).

The word "lusteth" is the Greek word *epipotheo*, and it describes *an intense desire, a craving, a hunger, an ache*, or *a yearning or hankering for something*. It could also be translated as *a longing* or *pining for something; to strain after, to greatly desire* or *to have strong affection*. This word *epipotheo* depicts a fervent passion or an obsession. It is actually the word used to describe a man who has an addiction to some type of drug or chemical. This addiction is so intense his body is bent over in convulsions, yearning and craving his next fix.

What's interesting is that in James 4:5, the one being described as having this intense craving and yearning — *epipotheo* — is the Holy Spirit, and He is hankering and longing for *you*! You are His "fix," and He is fervently passionate and obsessed with you. The fact is, He wants more of you today than yesterday, and tomorrow He will reveal another area in your life that He yearns to occupy and make new. As you yield your life to Him, He will fill you with more and more of Himself.

The Holy Spirit Is a Jealous Lover

In addition to the Holy Spirit's intense yearning for us, the Bible says He also experiences "envy." In Greek, the word "envy" is *phthonos*, which describes *jealousy*. It depicts *a hostile feeling toward someone else because of an advantage, benefit, or position that another has*. This is a deeply felt grudge due to someone possessing what one wishes was his own. The word *phthonos* also means to begrudge what another person possesses or to resent another person's possession or position and to try to find a way to seize it away from another person in order to make it his own.

This word "envy" — the Greek word *phthonos* — denotes *jealousy, ill will*, or *malice*. This is jealousy so strong that it tends toward *malice* and produces *envy*. This word *phthonos* is the very word that was used to illustrate the emotions of a young man who lost his lover and feels jealous for his old relationship to be restored. He most likely bears malice in his heart toward the romantic bandit and is envious of that relationship and wants it back.

What does the word *phthonos* — translated here as "envy" — have to do with us and the Holy Spirit? According to James 4:5, the Holy Spirit is a Divine Lover that is preoccupied with us. He wants to totally possess us and desires that our affections also be set on Him. When we walk and talk like unbelievers and give our attention and affection to other things, the Holy Spirit feels like a jealous Lover who has been robbed, and He wants His relationship with us to be restored. He has divine malice for the worldliness that has usurped His role in our lives. And He is filled with envy to see things put back the way they should be.

When you put all three words — *dwelleth*, *lusteth*, and *envy* — together, this paints quite a picture. Make no mistake: The Holy Spirit is not a passive partner. He aggressively and actively pursues us. He fiercely wants more of us! When we intentionally (or unintentionally) give any part of ourselves to something else or to someone else's control, the Holy Spirit will swing into action like a jealous Lover. He wants to seize what has been lost and bring it back under His divine control. He even has malice toward our preoccupation with other things.

It's true that we live in the world, work in the world, and function as human beings in the world. There's no way to get around that, and there's nothing wrong with going to work, buying a house, purchasing a new car, or enjoying new clothes. These things are needful in life. But we must keep these things in their proper place. The fact is, there are all kinds of things that can preoccupy our thinking. Sometimes it's just the cares of this life that pull us away from the Holy Spirit. We can get so busy — so committed to doing so many things — that it deteriorates our spiritual life. Amazing as it is, even good things in life, if taken to an extreme, can become adulterous in the eyes of the Lord. Only the Holy Spirit knows how to balance us.

In light of all we've discussed, James 4:5 carries this meaning:

> **The Spirit, who has come to settle down, make His home, and permanently dwell in us, has an all-consuming, ever-growing, excessive, passionate desire to possess us — and He is envious and filled with malice toward anything or anyone who tries to take His place in our lives.**

How Does the Holy Spirit Seek To Reestablish His Place of Preeminence?

The way that the Holy Spirit swings into action to regain our affection and restore His relationship with us is found in James 4:6, which says, "But he giveth more grace. Wherefore he saith, God resisteth the proud, but giveth grace unto the humble." The "proud" identified in this verse are Christians who are living wrong. They have drifted away from their devotion to God and have begun to give their affection and attention to other things. Their thinking and way of living is wrong, and because the Holy Spirit craves us so intensely, He goes to work to help these believers recognize their error and correct their course.

Specifically, the Bible says, "…God resisteth the proud…" (James 4:6). The word "resisteth" is a translation of the Greek word *antitassomai*, which means *to arrange oneself against* or *to methodically oppose*. It is a military term that depicts a strategic plan of opposition intended to bring a situation under control. The use of this word in the context of the verse tells us that God will arrange Himself against any erring believer. He will strategically oppose any Christian who is out of balance and off course with the purpose of bringing them back into a healthy, harmonious relationship with Himself.

Can you imagine anything worse than a Christian being opposed by God? The truth is, this opposition from God is an act of *grace*. It is God's Spirit bringing us into a place of brokenness — a place of *humility* — where sin is confessed and fellowship with Him is restored.

Therefore, the *humble* are the believers whose hearts seek to keep God — and the Holy Spirit — in first place in their lives. When they get out of balance and begin to be preoccupied with or chase other things, they receive the correction of the Holy Spirit and repent. They are quick to say, "Lord, I'm so sorry. I've done wrong. Please forgive me for putting other things before You in my life and grieving you. Retake Your rightful place, in Jesus' name." When we have this attitude of humility, the Holy Spirit is magnetically drawn to us!

Friend, if your priorities are out of line and you have drifted off course, receive the loving correction of the Holy Spirit. As you "draw nigh to God…he will draw nigh to you…" (James 4:8). When you come close to God and repent, the Holy Spirit will rush to where you are and wrap His loving arms around you. He will pour out His grace, which is His supernatural strength, and reinvigorate you with the very life of Christ! May you come to know the intimacy, the partnership, and the power of the Holy Spirit in your life like never before!

STUDY QUESTIONS

> Study to shew thyself approved unto God, a workman that needeth
> not to be ashamed, rightly dividing the word of truth.
> — 2 Timothy 2:15

1. Think for a moment: What are your thoughts focused on most of the time? On your *job*? On your *ministry*? On a particular *person*? On your *favorite hobby*? The answer to this question will probably tell you what consumes you most in life. If it's anything other than the Holy Spirit, how do you think He is going to respond? (Consider James 4:5,6 and the second half of First Peter 5:5.)

2. As strange as it seems, even good things in life, if taken to an extreme, can become adulterous in the eyes of the Lord. According to Scripture, anything that takes the place of God in your life is considered an idol. Meditate on this eye-opening word of instruction from the apostle John and ask the Holy Spirit to reveal any "idols" in your life you need to tear down:

   "Little children, keep yourselves from idols (false gods) — [from anything and everything that would occupy the place in your heart due to God, from any sort of substitute for Him that would take first place in your life]. Amen (so let it be)."
   — 1 John 5:21 (*AMPC*)

3. To help you avoid giving the Holy Spirit a reason to feel betrayed by or envious of other things in your life that have taken His place, take time each morning throughout the upcoming week to reflect on these words from the apostle Paul:

   "So here's what I want you to do, God helping you: Take your everyday, ordinary life — your sleeping, eating, going-to-work, and walking-around life — and place it before God as an offering. Embracing what God does for you is the best thing you can do for him. Don't become so well-adjusted to your culture that you fit into it without even thinking. Instead, fix your attention on God. You'll be changed from the inside out. Readily recognize what he wants from you, and quickly respond to it...."
   — Romans 12:1,2 (*MSG*)

PRACTICAL APPLICATION

But be ye doers of the word, and not hearers only,
deceiving your own selves.
—James 1:22

1. Have you ever experienced the intense desire and deep love of the Holy Spirit described in James 4:5? If you have, briefly describe your experience. Where were you, and what was going on in your life?

2. Prior to this lesson, had you ever seen the Holy Spirit as a jealous Lover who wants all of you to Himself? How does this truth change the way you see the Holy Spirit? How does it affect how you see your devotion to the things of this world?

3. Fact: You are as close to the Holy Spirit right now as you have chosen to be. The question is: Are you satisfied with where you are? If not, what do you need to do to experience a deeper, closer level of intimacy with Him? What practical steps can you take to make your relationship with the Holy Spirit top priority?

Notes